Jean Lyonnard

Perpetual intercession to the agonizing heart of Jesus

for the eighty thousand who die each day

Jean Lyonnard

Perpetual intercession to the agonizing heart of Jesus
for the eighty thousand who die each day

ISBN/EAN: 9783742860309

Manufactured in Europe, USA, Canada, Australia, Japa

Cover: Foto ©Lupo / pixelio.de

Manufactured and distributed by brebook publishing software (www.brebook.com)

Jean Lyonnard

Perpetual intercession to the agonizing heart of Jesus

PERPETUAL INTERCESSION

TO THE
AGONIZING HEART OF JESUS,

FOR THE
EIGHTY THOUSAND WHO DIE EACH DAY.

CONFRATERNITY-ASSOCIATION.

BY FATHER J. LYONNARD,
OF THE SOCIETY OF JESUS.

LONDON:
THOMAS RICHARDSON AND SON,
26, PATERNOSTER ROW;
9, CAPEL STREET, DUBLIN; AND DERBY.
NEW YORK: HENRY L. RICHARDSON AND CO.
MDCCCLXXI.

NIHIL OBSTAT.
Edmundus O'Reilly, S. J.,
Cens. Theol. Deput.

IMPRIMATUR.
Paulus Cardinalis Cullen,
Archiep. Dublinen.

Die 25 Aprilis, 1871.

CONTENTS.

CHAP.		PAGE.
	To the Reader ...	1
I.—	The Confraternity of the Agonizing Heart of Jesus ...	3
II.—	The Organization of the Confraternity of the Agonizing Heart of Jesus ...	7
III.—	Conditions of admission ...	9
	Act of Consecration, and promises to be made by the Associates on the day of reception ...	12
IV.—	Essential practices of the Confraternity: 1st. Duties of the Associates ...	14
	2nd. Duties of Companions ...	15
V.—	Of other practices in use in some Confraternities of the Agonizing Heart of Jesus	16
VI.—	Mode of establishing the Confraternity of the Agonizing Heart ...	20
VII.—	Motives for its establishment in parishes	21
VIII.—	Motives for its establishment in Religious Communities, hospitals, &c. ...	26
IX.—	Of Intercession in General ...	32
X.—	Of the daily Intercession ...	38
	Summary of what is done during the half hour of intercession ...	49

CONTENTS.

CHAP.		PAGE
XI.	Of the monthly Intercession	43
	Summary of what should be done at the monthly Intercession	47
XII.	Of the Annual Intercession	48
	Summary of what is to be done at the Annual Intercession	50
XIII.	Feasts of the Confraternity	52
XIV.	Of the Interior Spirit of the Intercession	55
XV.	Prayers which should be made at every time of Intercession	63
	Direction of the Intention	63
	Prayer to the Agonizing Heart of Jesus	65
	Prayer to the Compassionate Heart of Mary	66
	Litany of the dying	67
	Act of Reparation to the Agonizing Heart of Jesus	70
	Prayers for Associates and Companions, living and dead	72
	Act of Consecration to the Agonizing Heart of Jesus	74
XVI.	Other Prayers and Exercises which may also be used during the time of Intercession:	
	Devotion to the Agonizing Heart of Jesus	75
	Act of Reparation to the Compassionate Heart of Mary	77
	Act of Consecration to the Compassionate Heart of Mary	79
	Supplication to the Compassionate Heart of Mary	80
	Offering of our life for the Agonizing	81
	Prayer to St. Joseph, the Patron of a good death	81
	Prayer to the Guardian Angels of the dying	82

CONTENTS. ix

CHAP.		PAGE
Invocation of Jesus, Mary, and Joseph	...	83
Three Paters and Aves for the dying	...	83
Ejaculatory Offering of the Precious Blood		84
Prayer to Mary	...	84
Prayer to St. Michael, archangel, for the dying	...	85
Prayer to the angel who strengthened Jesus in His Agony, in the Garden of Olives	...	86
Another prayer to the guardian angels of the dying	...	86
Prayer to St. John the Evangelist, for the dying	...	87
Invocations	...	88
Praises of St. Gertrude to our Lord	...	88
Litany of the Sacred Heart ...	...	90
Litany of the Blessed Virgin ...	...	95
Invocations of St. Ignatius, *Anima Christi*		96
Another prayer of St. Ignatius, making offering of oneself to God ...	...	98
Invocations	...	98
Prayer to Jesus in His Agony, in honour of His Sweat of Blood in the Garden of Olives	...	99
Prayer to Jesus, in His Agony on the Cross		100
Prayer to Mary standing at the foot of the Cross	...	100
Another prayer to Mary, mother of Dolours		101
Recommendation to St. Joseph, patron of a good death	...	102
Recommendation to St. Michael, archangel, protector of souls	...	102
Psalm, Miserere	...	103
Benediction of the Blessed Sacrament	...	105

CONTENTS.

CHAP.		PAGE
	Ave Verum	106
	Veni Creator	107
	Hymn to the Sacred Heart	108
	Ave Maris Stella	110
	Sub tuum præsidium	111
	Stabat Mater	111
	Memorare	114
	Memorare of St. Joseph	115
	Prayer "En ego"	115
	Hymn in honour of the Agonizing Heart of Jesus	116
	Hymn in honour of the Compassionate Heart of Mary	120
XVII.—	The Holy Hour	123
	Confraternity of the Holy Hour	125
	Prayer which may be used during the Holy Hour	126
	Prayers of Blessed Margaret Mary Alacoque:	
	1. Act of Adoration to the Sacred Heart	127
	2. Consecration to the Sacred Heart	128
	3. Act of charity in contemplation of the Wound in the Sacred Side of Jesus	129
	4. Compact of Blessed Margaret Mary with the Sacred Heart	130
	5. To the Heart of Jesus	132
	Aspirations of love, by S. Mary Magdalen of Pazzi	133
XVIII.—	Easy Method of Meditation	135
	Meditations on the Agony of the Heart of Jesus in the Garden of Olives	138
	Meditation on the continual sufferings of the Heart of Jesus, during His whole mortal life	142

CONTENTS.

	PAGE
Method of hearing Mass in union with the Agonizing Heart of Jesus	148
Certificate of admission	167
Ticket of Intercession	167
Simultaneous exercise of Perpetual Intercession to the Agonizing Heart of Jesus, and of perpetual supplication to the Compassionate Heart of Mary	167
Daily Prayer to the Compassionate Heart of Mary for the hundred thousand children who are born each day	174
Ticket of Intercession and Supplication	175
Association of Voluntary Victims	175
Tickets of the Association of Voluntary Victims for the needs of the Church and the Nations, especially the Catholic Nations of Europe, in honour of the Agonizing Heart of Jesus, and the Compassionate Heart of Mary	178
1st. Ticket, The Church and France	179
2nd. Ticket, The Church and Italy	180
3rd. Ticket, The Church and Spain	181
4th. Ticket, The Church and Austria	182
5th. Ticket, The Church and Germany	183
6th. Ticket, The Church and England	184
7th. Ticket, The Church and Poland	185
8th. Ticket, The Church and Belgium	186
9th. Ticket, The Church and America	187
10th. Ticket, The Church, Asia, and Africa	188

TO THE READER.

We offer this little book to your pious consideration, hoping that you will kindly receive it with the same good will as its predecessors. It is the companion to the "Perpetual Supplication to the Compassionate Heart of Mary," which we published last year. Read and distribute them both, and remember that the zeal of the Christian ought always to be like a spreading flame. Do not content yourself with reading and getting others to read these books; but practise, and get others to practise what they contain. You will thus draw down the blessing of God on yourselves and your families, you will give glory to Jesus and Mary, you will promote the salvation of the dying, you will raise a barrier against the invasion of the *Solidaires*, that wicked band, whose mission it is to make men die as reprobates;[*]

[*] This sect arose in Belgium a few years ago, and has already gained a footing in many French towns. Let us do all we can to arrest its ravages.

you will comfort Holy Church, your mother, in her sorrows, and gain for her, from Heaven, fresh strength to conquer her enemies. May God, in His infinite mercy, make use of you, dear reader, for these glorious and holy ends, and may these little books help to forward them! We humbly offer them, like our others, to the agonizing Heart of Jesus, to the compassionate Heart of Mary, and to St. Joseph, the patron of a good death.*

According to a revelation made to a pious person, " our Lord looks with great favour on the Confraternity established in honour of His Agonizing Heart; many dying persons have already been saved by its intercessions; and their number will ultimately be counted, not by thousands, but by millions." This is not a matter of faith, but we who know the person to whom, and the circumstances in which the revelation was made, see no reason for doubt, and find in it great consolation. Glory be to God. Amen.

* We would call particular attention to an article at the end of this book, on "The Simultaneous Exercise of Perpetual Intercession to the Agonizing Heart of Jesus, and Perpetual Supplication to the Compassionate Heart of Mary."

PERPETUAL INTERCESSION
TO
THE AGONIZING HEART OF JESUS,

FOR THE EIGHTY THOUSAND WHO DIE EACH DAY.

We hope that the easy method which we are about to lay before the members of the Confraternity of the Agonizing Heart of Jesus, may assist them in the profitable employment of their appointed time of intercession for the dying. But we must begin by explaining the nature of the Confraternity.

CHAPTER I.

The Confraternity of the Agonizing Heart of Jesus.

The object of this Confraternity is, to honour the Sacred Heart of Jesus in the continual sorrows of His mortal life, especially in His Agony in the Garden of Olives; and, by the merits of that long agony, to obtain the grace of a good death for the *eighty thousand* who die *each day*. This number is not exaggerated, it is an ascertained fact.

The excellence and advantages of this Confraternity are obvious. Its special object of veneration is among the greatest, the holiest, the most perfect, that can be found in heaven or on earth, for it is the *Sacred Heart of Jesus*, considered in the most touching manifestations of Its love, in all that It has endured for our salvation; it is the *Agonizing Heart* of the only Son of God, equal to Him from all eternity; of the only Son of the Immaculate Virgin, born of her, in time, by the divine power of the Holy Spirit.

It meets the most urgent and important need of souls; of the countless multitudes who are dying each day. The eternal fate of thousands will be decided within the next *twenty-four hours*, a few minutes will seal that of a vast number. Alas! how many of them are in a state of mortal sin, and therefore on the very brink of hell! Can any need be greater than theirs? What can be more important than to beseech God, by the Holy Agony of Jesus, to show mercy to these poor creatures now in their agony? Hell is ready to swallow them up, will you not try to rescue them? Christians, pray, intercede for them. To-morrow it will be too late! In a few minutes, eternity will have begun for many of them.

The advantages of this Confraternity, and the motives for belonging to it, are weighty and numerous. In the first place, it offers a perpetual honourable reparation, a continual homage to the Agonizing Heart of Jesus. Those who love Him cannot but feel the power of such a motive. In the present day, the efforts of His love are often frustrated by the ingratitude and malice of His own children; justice calls upon us to make Him all the reparation in our power. In the second place, the Confraternity has already obtained, and will, we may hope, continue to obtain, countless graces for the dying. We can never duly appreciate these benefits, till we know, what the heart of man hath never known, what his eyes hath not seen, nor his ear heard; the ineffable happiness of heaven, the inexpressible misery of hell. An eternity of bliss! An eternity of torment! Joy or sorrow for ever! there is no alternative. The third motive is your own interest. If you can make some of your fellow-creatures happy for ever, will you not be amply rewarded? But there are many other advantages for members of this Confraternity; precious indulgences are attached to it, the excellent virtues of charity, zeal, confidence in God, and fear of His judgments, are called into practice; the spirit of faith and prayer is strengthened; the intention is purified; it opens to you an inexhaustible spring of grace and merit. The members of your families will experience its happy influence; and, above all, you will have great consolation at the hour of your death. How many hands and voices will there be raised, imploring God to grant the grace of a holy death to the charitable Christian who has often sought it for others! Do you think that the souls, to whom the gates of heaven have been opened by your prayers, can forget you in your last struggle? Oh! no, their intercession in heaven will be joined to those made for you by the Confraternity on earth. And how joyfully will they welcome you to join their blessed company for all eternity! Dear reader, one of your surest means of living a holy life and dying a holy death, is to do all you can for the agonizing. Pray for them; you will be prayed for in your turn when you are in your agony. And who knows how soon that may be?

CHAPTER II.

Organization of the Confraternity of the Agonizing Heart of Jesus.

Two classes of members compose this Confraternity, Associates and Companions. The former are the *working members*, and the *Association* consists exclusively of them. They are most closely united to the Confraternity, undertake to observe all its practices, and have a right to all its indulgences and privileges. *A public act of consecration to the Agonizing Heart of Jesus,* is pronounced by each, on the day of admission, in presence of the assembled associates. This act is accompanied by three promises, of which we shall speak hereafter. The Companions make no act of consecration and no promises; but their names are entered on the *Register of the Confraternity,* and they pray every day for the eighty thousand who die every day; they are thus united with the Associates, and gain a title to certain indulgences. The dignitaries are always chosen from among the Associates. Companions are not admitted to the common meetings of the Association, nor to the annual retreat made by its members, unless by a special permission from the Director and Council of the Confraternity.

The Director of the Association should be a fervent and intelligent priest, who will be careful to preserve its spirit, to promote the growth of its members in humility, piety, modesty, charity, zeal, and devotion, even more than the increase of their numbers; one who will faithfully watch over this little flock committed to him by the Good Shepherd; duly considering, in the sight of God, the fruits of salvation to be expected from each member, and his own great responsibility, since the earnestness of the Associates, and the efficacy of their prayers for the conversion and salvation of sinners, depend in great measure on his guidance.

The *Dignitaries* are chosen from amongst the Associates most distinguished by their virtues, their zeal and religious influence.

They are, the *president*, *vice-president*, or *assistant*, seven *counsellors*, one of whom is *first zelatrix*, and another *secretary*, and, lastly, a *treasurer*. We need not remind them of the care they should take to prove themselves worthy of the honour conferred upon them. Detailed *rules* regarding their different duties will be found in a little book called, "The Agonizing Heart of Jesus.—Statutes of the Association." (Le Cœur Agonizant de Jésus—Statuts de l'Association, chez Régis—Ruffet, Libraire Paris, Rue Saint Sulpice), which we beg the directors and dignitaries to procure. This book speaks merely of women, as an Association is generally composed of them; but, of course, men might also form one which ought to be perfectly distinct from the other.

CHAPTER III.

Conditions of admission into the Confraternity of the Agonizing Heart of Jesus.

This Confraternity consists, as we have said, of Associates and Companions. Any one desirous of becoming an Associate, should address a request for admission to the Director of the Confraternity, or to one of the chief dignitaries, who will submit it for approval to the Council of the Association; and, should no objection be made, the person then becomes a *postulant*. If, after a period of at least a month, the Council consider the postulant worthy, she is admitted to the Association, and makes *her act of consecration* to the Agonizing Heart of Jesus, publicly, in the chapel of the Confraternity, in presence of the other associates, adding the three following promises: first, to *pray every day for those who die that day;* secondly, to *make half an hour's intercession for the same intention, every month;* thirdly, *to assist at the meetings of the Association.* At the end of this chapter, we give the act of consecration, and the promises. They do not oblige under pain of mortal, or even venial, sin, but we earnestly beg those who have not a firm purpose of fulfilling them, to content themselves with remaining Companions of the Confraternity, instead of seeking admission as Associates. The duties of the Companions will be explained in the next chapter.

No one can become an Associate, who is not already a Companion: a person becomes a companion by having her name entered on the register of the Confraternity; to become an Associate, she must also, after admission by the Council, make the *public act of consecration*, and the *promises* of which we have spoken.

Any one who wishes to be a Companion, can send her name to the Director of the Confraternity; if no serious reason to the contrary exists, he enters it on the Register, and she can then, on fulfilment of the prescribed conditions, gain the indulgences granted to Companions. It will be seen that there is a great difference between the Associates and Companions, and it is most important that this difference should be maintained, otherwise the registers will soon be full of names, while the results in the promotion of the glory of God and the salvation of the dying will be small. We beg directors, and members of councils, to be very careful in their admission of associates; for, on their piety, devotion, and perseverance, the success of the Confraternity, and its influence for good in a neighbourhood, in great measure, depends.

FORM.

Act of Consecration, and Promises to be made by the Associates on the day of admission.

Adorable Heart of Jesus, Victim of love for the salvation of souls, I prostrate myself humbly before Thee, and, trusting in Thine infinite mercy, I consecrate myself for ever to Thy service, in this pious Association. I promise to honour, and to lead others to honour, the sorrows of Thy mortal life, and especially Thy holy Agony in the Garden of Olives, with a special worship. I promise to promote the salvation of the dying by my devotion and my prayers. In order to please Thee and to save them, I offer to Thee my body and soul, my joys and sorrows, my life and death, in union with Thy sufferings. O, Agonizing Heart of Jesus! deign to accept my humble homage, I place it under the protection of Thine Immaculate Mother. Presented by her pure hands, let it ascend to Thee as a sweet-smelling holocaust, and rise to the throne of Thy Heavenly Father, to whom, with Thee, in the Unity of the Holy Spirit, be honour and glory, world without end. Amen.

I engage myself by a simple promise, first, *to pray each day for those who die each day;* secondly, *to make half an hour's intercession each month for the same intention;* thirdly, *to assist at the meetings of the Association.*

Note.—1st. This form will be henceforth used in all our Confraternities for the admission of Associates. We beg the directors to omit no part of it. 2nd. Priests, and those in holy orders, monks and nuns, who wish to become Associates, can, on sending their names to the Director, receive permission to pronounce their act of consecration in any church, or any other place, provided only that some witnesses are present. They are not required to make the promises, nevertheless, they ought *faithfully to pray every day for the dying, and to make the half hour of intercession every month.* We beg priests, who are Associates, or even Companions, to say Mass from time to time, for the living and departed members of the Confraternity.

CHAPTER IV.

Essential practices of the Confraternity of the Agonizing Heart of Jesus.

I.—*Duties of the Associates.*

In virtue of their engagement, the Associates are bound: first, to say the prayer, "*O most merciful Jesus,*" at least, once every day, on behalf of the eighty thousand who die on that day. It would be well to say it three times a day, at morning prayer, at half past two in the afternoon, in honour of our Saviour's agony, and, in the evening, for those who are to die during the night. Associates who are unable to read or to learn the prayer, will say a *Pater* and *Ave* for the same intention.

Secondly, *to make half an hour's intercession, at least once a month,* for all who are to die *within twenty-four hours,* from the time when it is begun. This intercession should be made in the chapel of the Confraternity, from half past two to three o'clock in the afternoon, in honour of our Saviour's agony in the Garden of Olives and on the cross. We beg those who make it, also to pray for all who are to die before their half hour of intercession in the following month comes round.

Thirdly, *to assist at the monthly and yearly meetings of the Association*, in the chapel of the Confraternity, when the Associates offer their united intercessions for all who are to die during the coming month or year. We shall speak more fully hereafter of these meetings, and also of those held on the Feasts of the Association, which its members are bound to attend.

Such are the essential practices of the Associates; should any one be found negligent in their performance, it is the duty of the director and council to admonish her. If two or three admonitions fail, the unworthy member must be dismissed from the Association, and her name struck off its books. It is the duty of the Zelatrix to see that the Associates are faithful to their engagements, and to inform the director and council of negligence or omissions.

II.—*Duties of the Companions.*

The Companions are bound to say the prayer, *O most merciful Jesus*, at least once a day for the dying of the day; but we hope that they will adopt the practice of saying it three times a day, which we have suggested to the Associates. Those who cannot read nor learn the prayer should say a *Pater* and *Ave* for the same intention. The monthly half-hour of intercession is not binding on them, but we beg them to make it, and they ought to pray from time to time for the other Companions, as well as for the Associates, who in their turn pray for them at their meetings. They should pray most especially for any members of the Confraternity who are ill or dying, and, if possible, visit them and help them to die well.

CHAPTER V.

Of other practices in use in some Confraternities of the Agonizing Heart of Jesus.

The preceding chapter treats of fundamental and essential practices of the Confraternity, which must never be omitted; we are now about to speak of other practices in use in certain Confraternities, which, although neither fundamental nor essential, are very profitable, and well calculated to promote the objects in view. We hope that where it is possible, the Directors will encourage their observance.

The first is *visiting the sick and dying.* We need not enlarge on the excellence of this holy work of mercy, which is not only corporal but spiritual, since it directly promotes the eternal salvation of the dying. This indeed should always be the chief object, and every means for its attainment should be used. The visitors should be unwearied in good counsels, and generous and devoted services; they should also inform the priest of the state of the sick and dying, and endeavour to ensure their reception of the Sacraments, overcoming all difficulties which the negligence of relations and neighbours, or any other circumstances, may put in their way. They should mutually sustain and assist one another, so that where one has failed another may attempt the good work, and by God's blessing they will often have the consolation of seeing their efforts crowned with success. Let them constantly have recourse to the guardian angels of the sick and dying, to their patron saints, to the Compassionate Heart of our Lady, to St.

Joseph, the patron of a good death, to St. Michael the Archangel, guardian of souls, to the Angel who consoled Jesus in His agony in the Garden, and, above all, to Jesus Himself, and to His Agonizing Heart; and let them recommend the dying to the prayers of the Association, and especially of the members who are making the half-hour's intercession. We doubt not that the Directors will duly appreciate the advantages of this holy work, and we trust that their zeal will organize a system of visiting which shall include rich as well as poor. The subject should often be brought before the notice of the assembled associates, the most fervent of whom will gladly undertake such an employment. We beg them to do it for the love of the Agonizing Heart of Jesus, which has suffered so much, and has loved us so much; and for the sake of the countless multitude of the dying, of whom so many are in danger of eternal perdition. In a little book of ours, called "The Agonizing Heart of Jesus," * the Directors will find *statutes* for the organized visiting of the sick and dying.

* Le Cœur Agonisant de Jesus chez Régis. Buffet, Libraire à Paris, Rue Saint Sulpice.

The second practice which we recommend most strongly on account of its great efficacy, is, that each Associate should make a small annual offering, in order to have as many Masses as possible said for the dying throughout the world. One Confraternity, by means of these subscriptions, has a Mass said every day for this intention. The value of a single Mass is infinite, and who can tell how many may owe their eternal salvation to the graces thus obtained for them? Where it is found possible to establish the practice, the Zelatrix should collect the offerings in the month of January, and put them into the hands of the Treasurer.

The third practice is, that each Associate should go to Holy Communion once a month, on a different day, offering it for the dying, so that every day one or more Communions may be offered to God to gain the grace of a good death for those who are leaving this world.

It would be well to assign the same day for the Communion and the half-hour's intercession of each Associate. At the end of each month the Zelatrix should distribute tickets marking the day for intercession and Communion. Thirty-one Associates form a complete circle; the same Zelatrix may be at the head of several circles, and when a member is removed by death or any other cause, her place should be filled up as soon as possible.

CHAPTER VI.

Mode of establishing the Confraternity of the Agonizing Heart of Jesus.

Application must be made to the Bishop of the Diocese for the canonical erection of the Confraternity in any parish church or public chapel; he will the more readily grant such a request if the many advantages accruing to the faithful in general, to the dying, and to the church or community where the Confraternity is established, are fully laid before him. A Confraternity can apply for affiliation to the Archconfraternity of Jerusalem.

CHAPTER VII.

Motives for the establishment of the Confraternity of the Agonizing Heart of Jesus in parishes.

The Confraternity may be established with the greatest advantage in parish churches; first and most easily in those of large town parishes, and afterwards in country places. Death is everywhere: prayers for the dying are needed everywhere. In the present day innumerable dangers beset souls; the chances of a bad death, like the temptations to a bad life, are fearfully multiplied, and this spiritual work of mercy may prove to many a plank of salvation from shipwreck.

Venerable and zealous pastors of souls! how often have you been overwhelmed with grief when a dying person has rejected your ministry, or only accepted it in a formal manner, with cold indifference, wavering faith, uncertain contrition, and little or no sense of religion. How many times have you felt the need of some special assistance to break down the terrible barriers that close the door of souls against you, even to the last moment. Well, here is a powerful help in your ministry to the dying! Establish the Confraternity of the Agonizing Heart of Jesus in your parish. Choose as its first members a few devout persons on whose constancy and zeal you can rely; assemble them every month; make them thoroughly understand its nature, advantages, and practices. Lay particular stress on the practice of intercession. If the first nucleus does not number thirty-one persons, (and we recommend you to begin with fifteen or twenty,) do not require each to make the intercession more than once a month, unless they spontaneously offer to do so. But whether this holy exercise takes place daily, or only every second day, the associate who performs it should embrace in her intention all who are to die before the next associate's turn begins, so that the intercession may be unbroken.

Increase the number of associates very gradually; be very particular in your choice of persons. An association of thirty or forty really fervent persons will prove a far more valuable instrument for the salvation of the dying and the edification of your parish than a much larger but less devoted body. Their salutary influence will soon be seen in their own families and in the neighbourhood, more particularly if a system of visiting the sick and dying can be organized. Much good may be done by this means, not merely to the sufferers, but to their relations, many of whom are perhaps living without God. Can there be a more favourable opportunity of speaking of God, of giving good counsel to one who neglects religion, or warning a young person who is led astray by love of pleasure, than these visits of charity afford? The words spoken by your pious Associates to the sick and dying, to sorrowing parents, to desolate widows or bereaved children, may have a greater efficacy than all the eloquence of the preacher.

And do not say, "I have so many works on hand. So many associations are already established in my parish." O, dear brother, I should perhaps say so too, did I not know that even the best parishes are tainted with the impiety and corruption of the present day. The heart of a priest is full of compassion, like the Heart of Jesus; can it fail to be deeply moved at the thought that among the *eighty thousand who are dying each day*, the *three million who are dying each month*, the *thirty-six million who are dying each year*, multitudes are in a state of mortal sin, in danger of eternal ruin? The mercy of our Lord puts into your hands the means of assisting these poor souls in their great necessity; surely you will not fail to use them.

And, moreover, a great reward awaits you. Those who owe their eternal salvation to you, under God, will, when they are in heaven, repay you a hundred-fold what you have done for them on earth; they will pray for your parish, and they will pray for you when you are dying. What consolation in the thought! Alas! it sometimes happens that a priest who has borne to many the last aids of religion is himself suddenly struck down, and dies without them. Next to a good life, nothing can better ensure for you a good death than such zeal in the service of the dying as you will shew by establishing and maintaining this Confraternity in your parish.

With regard to the half-hour's intercession, although it is generally made from half-past two to three o'clock in the afternoon, yet another time may be chosen should any serious reason make it desirable. Field work in country places, and great heat in southern climates, will probably necessitate a change; but let the intercession be regularly made at some fixed hour, and in the chapel of the association. We attach great importance to the place, because, if any irregularity on this point is allowed, it would probably lead to unpunctuality and inexactitude in the intercession itself, so that the Association would fail to attain its object, and the dying would be deprived of the assistance they so much want. We cannot too strongly urge Directors and Zelatrixes to ascertain that each associate faithfully observes her appointed hour; in case of omission or negligence, if repeated admonitions are disregarded, the ticket of intercession must be withheld for one or two months from the offender, and should this privation fail to produce amendment, her name must be removed from the list of Associates. The same course should be adopted in regard of any associate whose conduct gives open scandal.

CHAPTER VIII.

Motives for the establishment of the Confraternity in religious communities, hospitals, etc.

The preceding chapter, though addressed to parish priests, is equally applicable to chaplains and superiors of religious houses and hospitals, &c. We beg you, therefore, dear brethren and sisters, to take it into consideration, and if your churches are favourably circumstanced, to endeavour to establish in them the Confraternity of the Agonizing Heart of Jesus, and to give the dying the great benefit of many fervent prayers and intercessions. How many poor souls will bless you throughout all eternity, for having rescued them from the devouring flames, and gained for them an entrance into bliss! What consolations and graces will be poured down upon your community! What a reward you will win if you establish and maintain this holy work, as far as your rule may permit, not only amongst people living in the world, but also amongst your religious, the children, the sick and infirm under their care!

Our Association cannot but find a home in the prayerful and quiet cloisters of the Carmelites, Poor Clares, Trappistines, and Benedictines, and their intercessions cannot fail to touch the Heart of Jesus, and gain pardon and grace for the dying.

And, in orders like the Ursulines and Visitandenes, the united prayers of mothers and children, of the nuns and their pupils, will have special charm for the Agonizing Heart of Jesus, and will be answered by special graces.

And, again, how gladly will the Association be hailed by hospital sisters, who have the spectacle of agony and death constantly before their eyes! Where can the need of consolation be more forcibly felt than in those asylums, where the sick, the infirm and the forsaken are gathered together? The Association of the Agonizing Heart of Jesus is specially calculated to meet their case. That Heart gives strength to the weak, support to the widow and orphan, patience to the aged and suffering. It enables the dying to meet their last conflict with courage, it gives them joy and hope to the end. Again, must not the need of a work of expiation and reparation be most deeply felt in hospitals, where the sisters are so often brought face to face with hardened sinners, far more diseased in soul than even in body? Let me appeal directly to their testimony. Is it not true, my dear sister, that you have more than once seen these sad sights? Is it not true, that among the many sick and dying, on whom you lavish your charitable care, by night and by day, some have wounded your heart by their indifference, or even by their impiety and their blasphemies, when on the very threshold of eternity? "Alas!" you answer, "it is but too true! not once, but often, have I witnessed these grievous scenes, and have been overwhelmed with grief at the thought that in a few hours, or moments, there will be another lost soul in hell!" And does not this make you realize the need of a work of expiation, reparation, and mediation, which may come to the rescue in cases where even your charity and the zeal of the minister of Christ have proved unavailing to touch a heart of stone? And this devotion, which presents to our worship the eminently expiatory mystery of our Lord's

Agony in the Garden of Olives, is essentially a work of expiation. Establish the Confraternity in your church, above all, let the daily intercession be made. Does a single day ever pass in great hospitals, during which the good sister has not to stand by a death-bed? Thank God, all the dying are not in the bad dispositions of which we have spoken, but all have need of prayers in that awful hour when the devil makes his last and most terrible attack on the departing soul, and then, how many among them have to look back on a guilty past, and to repair years, or even a whole life of sin, by a sincere confession and true penitence! We cannot but repeat it, if the work we advocate ought to find a place anywhere, it surely is in hospitals and asylums; and it would be well if every hospital, especially in large towns, could have the Confraternity, with all its practices, regularly established in its church.

Do not say, "How shall we find time in a hospital for the half hour of intercession every day?" for, in the first place, each person's turn will come but once a month; you will find no difficulty in forming amongst the sisters, and the sick, the poor, and the orphans, under their care, a circle of at least thirty-one persons, each of whom will make intercession for the dying in general, and for those in the hospital in particular, on an assigned day, before the picture of the Agonizing Heart, in the Confraternity Chapel; and, secondly, you can choose any half hour in the day that may suit you, or, if no other time is free, you can devote a part of your morning or evening meditation to this pious exercise.

Cloistered Contemplative orders, like the Carmelites and Poor Clares, and those which lead a life at once contemplative and active, like the Visitandines and Ursulines, can easily establish the practice of daily intercession in their monasteries, and they need not fear that they are departing from the spirit of their institute, in devoting some of their time to the dying, for whom the Son of God shed the last drop of His Blood. Pray for them, then, and others will pray for you when you are in your agony.

Important note regarding cloistered and other communities, asylums, hospitals, etc.—If no confraternity of the Agonizing Heart is established in a Community Church, any members of the Community who wish to enter the Confraternity should send their names to the Director of a Confraternity elsewhere, asking to be registered as companions, but if they wish to become associates the following particulars must be observed.

1st. In the case of nuns, they need merely ask to have their names entered as Associates, a Superior can make this request for all her nuns, and at the same time she ought to ask permission for herself and for them to make the *act of consecration* in the church of their community; the director will readily grant it, and on pronouncing the act in each other's presence, they become *Associates*.

2nd. The names of any among the pupils, the sick or poor in a convent, who are worthy to become Associates may be sent to the Director in the same manner, with a similar request regarding the act of consecration; if such persons afterwards leave the Convent, they should seek re-admission into the Confraternity, and make their act of consecration in the usual way in the Confraternity Church.

We will conclude this important chapter, by relating an edifying fact. The Lord, who chooses the instruments of His Mercy from all classes of society, has inspired a fervent layman in one of the largest towns of France with a great desire to devote himself to the dying in the Hospital of the town. Every month he makes a short report of the state of these poor souls, and begs the prayers of some pious persons for them; the next month he makes known the results obtained. God is pleased to reward the faith and piety of this generous Christian, and remarkable conversions often console him and his fellow-labourers. While these reports attest the charity of their good author, they also give a melancholy picture of the corruption and perversity too common in the souls of the sick and dying, and show the necessity for a holy crusade of prayer on their behalf.

CHAPTER IX.

Intercession in General.

Three exercises of intercession are in use in this Association; *daily intercession* for *the eighty thousand who die each day;*

monthly intercession for the three millions who die each month; and *annual intercession for the thirty-six millions who die each year.* But before speaking of each of these exercises in particular, let us say a few words on the subject in general.

Intercession for the dying is Devotion to the Agonizing Heart of Jesus reduced to practice; it is the principal exercise of our Association; the person who intercedes should begin by *honouring the Agonizing Heart of Jesus in all the sorrows of His mortal life,* and more particularly *in His Agony in the Garden;* and should then *beg Jesus, by the merits of that agony, to grant the grace of a good death to all the dying who are to pass into eternity in the interval between her intercession and the next.* The intercession will thus be continuous; and as people are every moment going to appear before the tribunal of Almighty God, it is most necessary that fervent intercessions should constantly arise to appease His anger and obtain for them the grace of a good death.

Intercession for those in their agony is an excellent work.

To enter into its excellence, we need only consider the meaning of the word; to *intercede* means to *interpose oneself* by humble, fervent and importunate prayer, between the thousands of sinners who are about to die, and God who is about to judge them; it means to draw near to the Divine Redeemer with lowly and fervent entreaties, beseeching Him of His infinite mercy to apply to these thousands the merits of His Sufferings, His Agony and His Death; to open to them His loving Heart, to place them there as in an ark of safety, and to bring them to the port of a blessed eternity. Is not this one of the most excellent, most apostolic and most divine works that a Christian can perform? Is it not the work of Christ Himself, the Mediator, the great *Intercessor?*

When our Lord was on this earth, He made intercession for us by His prayers and His Sacrifice of Himself on the Cross; in the Holy Sacrament of the Altar, He intercedes for us by His prayers, and by His unbloody Sacrifice; and in heaven He still intercedes for us by praying, by showing to God the Father the marks of His Wounds, and by offering to Him a perpetual sacrifice of praise and love.

Surely every member of Christ would gladly unite his intercessions to those of his Divine Head!

Pious souls, who take part in this holy work, esteem yourselves highly favoured in having so sublime a mission, in being companions of Jesus in His Agony, and performing for Him the office of the Angel of Consolation. Think it an honour to plead the cause of the dying. O! how important an affair is entrusted to you! You may be said to hold the eternal fate of thousands in your hands.

Intercession for the dying is a very holy work.

St. Paul, speaking of Jesus Christ, says, "It was fitting that we should have such a High Priest, holy, innocent, undefiled, separated from sinners." *Talis enim decebat ut nobis esset Pontifex sanctus, innocens, impollutus, segregatus à peccatoribus.* (Heb. vii.) Our great High Priest is heard because of

His Holiness; would you be heard when you intercede for those in their agony? Then be holy, innocent, and undefiled. Flee all sin, above all mortal sin. Before beginning your intercession take care to purify your conscience, by an act of deep humility and perfect contrition. And as by yourself you can do nothing, unite yourself to the holy intentions of Jesus in the prayers for the dying which He made on Mount Olivet, and still makes on the Altar. Unite yourself to the intercessions of the Compassionate Heart of Mary. Unite yourself to St. Joseph, the patron of a good death; to St. Michael, the archangel who overcame the infernal dragon; to the holy guardian angels of the dying for whom you pray; to their patron saints; to the Angel of the Agony, to St. John the Evangelist, and St. Mary Magdalen, who stood beneath the Cross. Unite yourself to the happy souls who have been saved by the intercessions of the Confraternity; to all priests who shall say Mass throughout the whole world within the next twenty-four hours, especially to those who shall say it in the Church where you are praying. Finally, unite yourself to all Confraternities of the Agonizing Heart, and more particularly to those members who make intercession at the same time as you do.

Your deficiencies in humility, patience, charity, fervour, confidence in God, and all the other virtues needed to make you an intercessor pleasing to the Heart of Jesus, will thus be supplied. If you should unhappily fall into mortal sin, do not on that account omit your intercession, but humble yourself, make an act of perfect contrition and a promise to our Lord that, as soon as you can, you will go to Confession.

Bear in mind that your intercession is the continuation of our Lord's prayer and intercession in the Garden of Olives. When you are on your knees interceding for the agonizing, Jesus Christ, your Divine Head, is interceding in you, is uniting your intercession to His own, and offering it to His Heavenly Father on your behalf and on theirs. What an honour and favour for you! What a powerful incentive to your zeal is the confidence that God places in you by condescending to let you be associated with His Beloved Son in His ministry of reconciliation!

O then perform your holy duty with all possible fervour! How many souls may owe their salvation to your intercessions, and bless you for ever for having rescued them from hell! But make yourself worthy to be heard. The more holy your life, the more will you resemble the great Intercessor, and the more efficacious will be your prayers for the dying!

CHAPTER X.

Of the Daily Intercession.

The *daily intercession* is generally made from half-past two to three o'clock in the Chapel of the Confraternity, by one or more members of the Association, appointed in turn, so that each one may take part in it, at least once a month. As we have said, this intercession should be made, with the intention of honouring the Agonizing Heart of Jesus, and of obtaining a good death for the eighty thousand who are to die during the twenty-four hours which will elapse before the next intercession. The next day at the same hour, another Associate will pray for the dying of the *following* twenty-four hours. By this means, all who die, at any hour of day or night, share the intercessions of the Association. Beware, then, lest by your omission of this holy exercise, or your negligence in its performance, you should deprive the dying of the assistance on which their eternal welfare may depend!

When your half hour of intercession is over, look on yourself as still specially entrusted by the Association, with the interests of those for whom you have just been praying, and continue to act as their intercessor until half-past two the next afternoon. In order to do this, it is not necessary to give up any of your usual occupations, you need only, before leaving the Church, direct your intention, by offering to the Agonizing Heart of Jesus your works and your sufferings. Renew this intention from time to time, often recommending these precious souls to the compassionate Heart of Mary, to St. Joseph the patron of a good death, to St. Michael the archangel, that he may defend them against the infernal dragon, to their guardian angels, to the angel who strengthened our Lord in His Agony, to their patron saints, to St. John the Evangelist and St. Mary Magdalen, who assisted at our Lord's death, to the good thief, who, at the point of death, heard from His lips the consoling word, "*To-day shalt thou be with me in Paradise;*" say the prayer, *O most merciful Jesus*, several times through the day, and especially before you lie down to rest, for those who are to die during the night, and offer your sleep to Jesus for them.

The exercise of *daily intercession* may be thus summed up: each Associate should, on an assigned day of the month, make intercession from half-past two to three o'clock, in the Confraternity Chapel, for those who are to die before half-past two o'clock the next day; and should also continue in a spirit of intercession for them, during this whole time, in the manner which we have explained. It would be well for each Associate to go to Communion for the dying on the day of her Intercession, and to prepare for the intercession a day or two beforehand, by special recollection, modesty, humility, mortification and charity, by increased fervour and careful avoidance of sin.

We beg the Associates every day at half-past two o'clock, to spend a moment in recollection, so as to unite themselves with those who are then beginning their intercession in the Church, and even to spend this half hour in a *spirit of intercession*, by offering their intention without interrupting their ordinary occupations. It would of course be still better if they could daily make half an hour's or even a quarter of an hour's intercession, but all have not the time nor the attraction for this.

The spirit of our Confraternity would have suggested the time of our Lord's Agony in the Garden as the fittest for the daily intercession, but the lateness of the hour is an insuperable objection to many persons, and we have therefore chosen the time of the Agony on the Cross. But we beg the Associates occasionally to practise the Devotion of the Holy Hour in their own houses; this pious exercise was recommended to Blessed Margaret Mary Alacoque by our Lord Himself, as a way of honouring His Agony in the Garden. We shall speak of it more fully in a later chapter. The *Agony in the Garden* is the principal object proposed to the homage of the Associates during their time of intercession, but the Agony of our Lord on the Cross, and His interior agonies during the whole course of His mortal life, must never be forgotten by them.

Note.—One or more *prie-Dieu* chairs should be placed in the Confraternity Church, and some cards with the prayers to be used during the time of intercession, very legibly written on them. All the prayers in chapter XV. should be given in their order, and some, if not all of those in chapter XVI. The act of honourable reparation, and of consecration to the Compassionate Heart, should not be omitted.

SUMMARY

Of what is to be done in the half-hour of Intercession.

1st. Let it be made regularly in the Confraternity Chapel, before a picture of the Agonizing Heart of Jesus, from half-past two to three o'clock in the afternoon of the day appointed.

2nd. Begin by adoring the Most Holy Sacrament; make an act of humility and of contrition for all your sins; unite yourself to the intentions, prayers and sufferings of the Agonizing Heart of our Lord, especially in the Garden of Olives, and to those of the Compassionate Heart of Mary.

3rd. Say the prayers given in Chapter

XV.; as all these prayers should be said, it is well to begin with them.

4th. Any of the prayers in Chapter XVI., may then be used, or you can meditate on the mystery of our Saviour's Agony in the Garden, on the sufferings of His mortal Life, etc., offering your meditation for the salvation of the dying.

CHAPTER XI.

The Monthly Intercession.

The Monthly Intercession is generally made in the afternoon of the last Friday of the month, in the Confraternity Church, and should be attended by all the Associates. Its object is to give solemn honour to the Agonizing Heart, and to gain the grace of a good death for about three millions who will die in the course of the following thirty-one days. Do not fail to attend this exercise; let these three millions have the benefit of your prayers in their agony; who can say for how many of them they may obtain eternal happiness?

The Director, or in his absence a zelatrix, begins this exercise by announcing the intention for which it is made, viz.: the honour of the Agonizing Heart and the good death of the three millions who are to die within a month,* some prayers are then said in an audible voice, and all present should respond. After these prayers the Director gives the Associates an instruction on some subject calculated to increase their Devotion to the Agonizing Heart of Jesus, to lead them to imitate His virtues, especially His *humility;* to quicken their zeal for the salvation of the dying, to strengthen their faith, to give them a greater love of prayer, or to make them more faithful to the duties of their station, more self-denying, fuller of love to God and man, of devotion to our Lady of Compassion, and to St. Joseph, the patron of a good death. He should often speak to them of our Blessed Lord, of His different titles, His virtues, His immense love for mankind, His suffering Life, His Agony, His Death, and His Presence in the Blessed Eucharist, that they may learn to love Him more. He should often place before them the great Intercessor as their model, and remind them

* See the beginning of Chapter XV.

that He is our Head, and we His members, and that our prayers, actions and sufferings in union with His, have Divine efficacy both for ourselves and for others, and that great purity of intention is therefore incumbent upon us. The comparison of the Vine and the branches, by which our Saviour explains our relation to Him, will also form a fitting theme of instruction. *Ego sum vitis vos palmites.* From time to time it will be well to impress upon the Associates, the importance of great regularity in their intercession, and as daily meditation is a sure means of advancing in holiness, the manner of making it might be explained. The instruction will be followed by an act of honourable reparation to the Agonizing Heart of Jesus, and by Benediction of the Blessed Sacrament.

At the close of the monthly exercise the zelatrix should distribute the tickets of intercession for the next month; the form of these tickets will be given at the end of this book, and copies should be printed. Where the practice of making a Communion every month for the dying is established, each Associate's day should be indicated on her ticket.

On the day of the Monthly Intercession, Mass is said for the Associates living and dead, and for all persons who are to die within a month. The Associates should assist at the Mass, and if possible go to Communion for each other and for the dying. The collections made on Festivals and at the meetings of the Confraternity, with the alms and subscriptions, will suffice for these masses as well as for the other expenses of the Association.

This monthly Mass might be preceded by a meditation, the director, or a zelatrix from time to time giving the different points.

During the Mass and at the evening ceremony, hymns should be sung. A harmonium will be most useful on these occasions, for sacred music has great power to raise the heart to God; the associates who undertake the charge of this part of worship will find full scope for their zeal and devotion, and for the exercise of a true apostolate. The angels in heaven constantly sing the praises of God, and must there not be angels on earth to sing His praises and those of His Divine Son?

SUMMARY

Of what should be done at the Monthly Intercession.

1st. Mass is said for Associates living and dead, and for all who are to die before the next monthly intercession. Assist at this Mass and offer your communion for the same intentions.

2nd. In the evening the exercise of intercession takes place as follows: 1, A hymn is sung; 2, The director in a surplice, in the pulpit or at the foot of the altar, says aloud the prayers given in Chapter XV., omitting the acts of honourable reparation and of consecration to the Agonizing Heart of Jesus. In the director's absence, the president or the first zelatrix says these prayers. 3, An instruction, act of honourable reparation to the Agonizing Heart of Jesus, Benediction of the Blessed Sacrament, immediately followed by a Pater and Ave for the sick and dying specially recommended to the Association. The intention of this Pater and Ave should be announced, so that all the Associates may join in it.

CHAPTER XI.

Of the annual Intercession.

The annual Intercession takes place on the Tuesday or Friday after Septuagesima, being (in different places respectively) the Feast of the Prayer of our Lord on Mount Olivet. It should be made with all possible solemnity and splendour, but let the Associates always remember that lively faith, fervent devotion to our Lord in the Blessed Sacrament, compassion for His Agony, and union with His prayers for the dying, are more precious offerings in His sight, than any earthly treasure.

The *annual intercession* seeks to give all possible honour to the Agonizing Heart of Jesus, and to obtain the grace of a good death for about thirty-six millions who will die within the year. Again let us urge the Associates to give this multitude the benefit of their intercessions. How many of them are in mortal sin! How many may be saved by fervent prayer!

The *annual intercession* is made in the Confraternity Church, which should be adorned as richly as possible, above all, about the altar and the picture of the Agonizing Heart. This picture should occupy a conspicuous place, and lights should burn before it all day, and especially at the closing ceremony in the evening.

On the morning of this beautiful Feast, Mass will be said for associates and companions living and dead, and for all who are to die throughout the whole world within a year; the associates should assist at the Mass, and go to Communion for the same intentions.

All through the day, until the end of the evening ceremony, uninterrupted intercession should be kept up; one associate or more in turn, spending a certain time, say half an hour, in presence of the Blessed Sacrament exposed on the altar, and before the picture of the Agonizing Heart. The intention of each during her intercession will be the honour of the Agonizing Heart and the salvation of those who are to die within a year. The zelatrix should distribute tickets beforehand, marking each person's time of intercession; some of the most fervent companions may be admitted on this occasion.

In the evening there will be a sermon,

followed by solemn acts of consecration, and of honourable reparation to the Agonizing Heart of Jesus, and by Benediction of the Blessed Sacrament. The singing of hymns, both at Mass and at the evening ceremony, will help to do honour to this Feast.

A *triduum* of prayers would be a fitting preparation for the annual Intercession; the director of each Confraternity can best regulate the order and number of exercises. A meditation before Mass, and an instruction in the evening would be found most profitable, and all Associates ought to attend. We mean to publish some meditations on the Sorrows of the Agonizing Heart of Jesus, and of the Compassionate Heart of Mary, which may be useful on these occasions.

SUMMARY

Of what is to be done at the Annual Intercession.

The *annual intercession* differs from the monthly intercession only by its greater solemnity, and by the continued intercession throughout the day. The *annual Mass* is said in the Confraternity Church, for *Associates and Companions, living and dead,* and for all persons who are to die within a year. Associates should assist at this Mass, and go to Communion for the same intentions. The Blessed Sacrament should, with the Bishop's permission, be exposed during the whole day. *The act of consecration* to the Agonizing Heart, and the *promises* are renewed in the evening in the name of the Association, by the president accompanied by her assistant. She kneels with a lighted candle in her hand before the picture of the Agonizing Heart, or at the Sanctuary rails, and pronounces them aloud, in the plural. This renewal is again made on the Feast of the Sacred Heart, under whose Patronage the Confraternity is placed; if hereafter his Holiness should sanction a special Feast of the Agonizing Heart it would become the principal Feast of the Confraternity.

Note.—On the Feasts of the Confraternity, as well as on the days of monthly and annual Intercession, candles should be kept burning before the picture of the Agonizing Heart. Every day during the half-hour's intercession two should be lighted before it.

CHAPTER XIII.

Feasts of the Confraternity.

The principal Feast of the Confraternity is that of the Sacred Heart of Jesus, after the Octave of Corpus Christi. It should be very solemnly celebrated by Mass and a general Communion of the Associates, followed in the evening by sermon, renewal of the act of consecration and the promises, solemn act of reparation to the Agonizing Heart, and Benediction of the Blessed Sacrament. If Exposition of the Blessed Sacrament is permitted, the zelatrixes will arrange the order in which the Associates will make constant adoration during the day. The two secondary Feasts of the Confraternity are the Patronage of the Blessed Virgin and of St. Joseph. We beg Associates to observe them devoutly, going to Holy Communion at the Confraternity Mass, and in the evening to Sermon and Benediction. The Compassionate Heart of our Lady should always

THE AGONIZING HEART OF JESUS. 53

be an object of special Devotion to them, but more than ever on the day consecrated by the Church to the memory of her Dolours. The other Patrons of the Confraternity are, St. Michael the Archangel, (September 29,) St. John the Evangelist, (December 27,) St. Camillus of Lellis, (July 18,) St. Mary Magdalen of Pazzi, (June 3,) St. Aloysius Gonzaga, (June 21.) Let us often, and particulary on their Feasts, invoke their protection for the Association and for the dying.

Note.—1. It is the custom in one of our Confraternities for the members to wear, on special occasions, a medal of the Agonizing Heart, given to them on the day of admission; this practice might with advantage be made general.* Each Associate should have a certificate of admission, which will serve both as a remembrance and as an incentive to fervour.† The list of Associates should be hung up in the Confraternity Chapel.

2. Postulants approved by the Council,

* These medals may be had in Paris, from Mayaud, frères, boulevard Sebastopol 11.

† The form of a certificate is given at the end of this volume. Copies should be printed.

after a trial of at least a month, will be publicly received on one of the Feasts of the Association. The day of annual intercession is to be preferred, but it may be done on any of the Secondary Feasts. During the Confraternity Mass, (at which they should communicate,) immediately after the Elevation, they will pronounce their act of consecration and their promises aloud, kneeling before the picture or the Altar, accompanied by the President or the Assistant, and holding a lighted candle. If many Postulants are to be received at once, the acts, etc. may be begun at the Offertory. Each Postulant must make them, unless she is unable to read, in which case the President says them in her name, and she answers, Amen. This act is the *indispensable condition* of admission into the Association.

CHAPTER XIV.

Of the interior spirit of the Intercession.

The interior spirit and dispositions of which we are about to speak, are the *soul* of the intercession; while the vocal prayers and other pious exercises form its *body*. Evidently the best possible spirit which we can bring to this holy work, is the one which unites us most closely to our Lord in His prayers and intercessions in the Garden of Olives.

First disposition: *Union with Jesus on His way to the Garden of Olives.* The grotto of the Agony was outside the city of Jerusalem; our Lord had to walk some distance to get there. As He went along He held holy and tender converse with His disciples; His heart was already full of grief, and He said to them, "My soul is sorrowful even unto death:" *Tristis est anima mea usque ad mortem.*

Associates of the Agonizing Heart, as you go to the Confraternity Church to make your intercession, unite yourselves to that holy sorrow of your Lord, which was caused less by the cruel Agony He was about to undergo than by the ingratitude and the sins of men; lay yours amongst the number. If the Church is at a distance from your abode, if it is *outside* the town, be glad that you, like Jesus, have a long way to go to the Garden of Olives, for the Church ought to be to you like Gethsemani and the Grotto of the Agony.

As you leave your house, then, imagine yourself to be going forth with Jesus, hear Him say to you, as of old to His disciples, "*My soul is sorrowful even unto death.*" Place yourself with the three disciples who followed Him into the garden. Unite yourself to the holy dispositions of His Heart. Say to yourself as you go along, I am going to bear my Jesus company in His Agony, I am going to console His most loving Heart, in its sadness and desolation and Agony. I am going to unite my intercession to His. I am going to pray to Him on behalf of the dying, for whom He prayed, and for whom He suffered. Take courage, my soul! Let us go and comfort Jesus; let us go and pray with Him; let us, if it be His will, go and suffer with Him and die with Him! *Eamus et nos ut moriamur cum eo.* (John, xi.) Alas! among these thousands and millions for whom I am going to intercede, how many are in the greatest danger of hell! Let us do our best to rescue them. Jesus! Mercy!

When you kneel down to adore Jesus on the Altar or to venerate His picture, think you see Him before you, pointing with one hand to His Agonizing Heart, and with the other to the multitudes who are about to appear before the tribunal of God, and hear Him saying to you; *Vigilate et orate :* Watch and pray. Do not sleep like the disciples, do not deserve the reproach, "Could you not watch one hour with me?" but be more watchful and fervent than you have ever been before. Unite yourself with great humility, contrition and confidence to Jesus in His prayer and Agony, and begin your intercession.

Second disposition. Union with Jesus in His prayer and Agony in the Garden of Olives. In the Grotto of the Garden Jesus is *alone, He prays, and He suffers.* During your intercession, be *alone, pray and suffer.*

1st. *Be alone*, that is to say, be as if there were no one but Jesus and you in the Church, humble yourself most deeply before God, like Jesus prostrate on His Face. Do not let the presence of others interfere with your humility and recollection, beware of yielding to any distraction, it is not the time or place for it. The place is holy, the Son of God is really present on the Altar, you are under His eye, you have come to honour His divine Heart in the Sorrowful Mystery of His Agony, and to ask for mercy for countless mortals in their agony; thousands of them will be in eternity even before the half hour of your intercession has come to an end. Can you let negligence or distractions waste the precious moments when you might be gaining salvation for so many? Can you think of anything but of the mission with which you are entrusted?

2nd. *Pray, intercede.* This is what you have come to do; the work the Association has entrusted to you. Try to represent it worthily. Remember that by yourself you can do nothing, that your prayers will be of no avail unless they are offered in the name of Jesus. Pray in His name, intercede in union with the Intercession for the dying which He made in the Garden of Olives. Offer to God the Father the prayer of His Agonizing Son. Beg our Lady of Compassion to be your advocate with her Divine

Son, and then you cannot but be heard, and your prayer, sanctified by its union with the prayers and intercessions of Jesus and Mary, will save souls in agony.

3rd. *Suffer.* Jesus not only prayed in the Garden of Olives, He suffered, and what suffering! He agonized, and what mortal agony! *"Being in an agony, He prayed the longer," Factus in agoniâ prolixiùs orabat.* After the example of the innocent Lamb of God, add suffering to your prayer, there is no surer means of making it efficacious on behalf of the dying. Before the day of intercession, and still more on the very day, prepare yourself by some voluntary sacrifice; take special pains to conquer self, to correct your failings, to practise mortification. If you are in the habit of using some instrument of penance, choose the day and if possible the time of your intercession for doing so; you will thus carry out in some measure that which is said of our Lord, *"Being in an agony, He prayed the longer."* But above all, let your will be in perfect submission to the Will of God, and ready for any sacrifice, even that of life itself, should He require it. This was the disposition of Jesus in His Agony in the Garden.

Oppressed with anguish, bowed down with sorrow, and overwhelmed with agony, Jesus is resigned, like a gentle Lamb led to the sacrifice; He makes His complaint, or rather His humble and submissive prayer to His Father, "*Father, if Thou wilt, remove this chalice from me; but yet not My will, but Thine be done:*" *Pater si vis, transfer calicem istum à me; verumtamen non mea voluntas, sed tua fiat.* (Luke, xxii.) See His readiness to suffer and to die for the glory of God, and the salvation of men. Be ready, by the help of His grace, to accept every thing from God's Hand, sorrow or joy, sickness or health, death or life, for His greater glory and for the salvation of the dying. If God asked of you, as He did of His Divine Son, the sacrifice of life on their behalf, would you refuse to make it? Surely, not. Say then, with Jesus, from the bottom of your heart, *Father, if Thou wilt, remove this chalice from me: but yet not My will but Thine be done.*

Third disposition. *Union with Jesus, continuing in prayer and in agony.* Persevere after the example of Jesus; be faithful in the performance of the various exercises of intercession. Never omit the monthly half hour unless it is absolutely impossible for you to keep it, and in such a case be sure to give notice to the zelatrix, that she may provide some one to take your place. But, we beg you never to do this except in case of real necessity. If you were told, that the Sovereign Pontiff, the Vicar of Christ, would to-day admit you to an audience, and grant many blessings and favours to you and your family, would you ask any one else to go instead of you? Certainly not; but now it is Jesus Christ Himself, the only Son of God, your Creator, your Redeemer, who invites you to an audience, who asks you to bear Him company in the Grotto, where He suffered and prayed so much for you! He says to you, "Come, My child, come and compassionate My agony, the sorrows of My soul, and the anguish of My Heart. Come and honour the Sweat of Blood I shed for you. Come and pray with Me. I will heap blessings upon you and your family, upon the Association of which you are a member, upon the dying for whom you intercede."

Such is your good Master's invitation, surely you will not let another accept it instead of you? It would seem as if you did not understand the immensity of His favours, or were unwilling to give Him the proof of love which He asks of you. Rather, when your turn comes, hasten to secure the blessings which the Heart of Jesus is ready to pour upon you.

Draw near to the Agonizing Heart, seek salvation for your brethren from that never-failing spring. Say constantly, "O Jesus, I pray Thee by Thine Agonizing Heart, have pity on the dying, show them mercy, preserve them from hell. O Mary, I pray Thee by Thy Compassionate Heart, have pity on the dying, obtain mercy for them, preserve them from hell. St. Joseph, patron of a good death, St. Michael, archangel, holy guardian angels, Saints in heaven, have pity on the dying, defend them, intercede for them, preserve them from hell!"

Note.—It is desirable that in every Church where the Confraternity is established, there should be a picture of the Agonizing Heart, before which the Associates may make their intercession.

CHAPTER XV.

Prayers which should be made at every time of Intercession.

These are, 1st, the direction of the intention, followed by the Lord's prayer and the Hail Mary; 2nd, the prayer to the Agonizing Heart of Jesus and the Compassionate Heart of Mary for the dying, with the Invocations; 3rd, the litany of the dying; 4th, the act of honourable reparation to the Agonizing Heart of Jesus; 5th, the prayers for the Associates and Companions living and dead. The act of consecration to the Agonizing Heart of Jesus may be added. We give these prayers in the order in which they should be used.

Direction of the Intention.*

(Always to be made before beginning the Intercession.)

In the Name of the Father, and of the Son, and of the Holy Ghost. Amen.

---

* The dying are in the most urgent need of prayers, for in a few hours they must appear before the tribunal of God,

At the daily intercession. Let us honour the Agonizing Heart of Jesus and the Compassionate Heart of Mary. Let us intercede for about *eighty thousand*, who are to die within the next *twenty-four* hours, especially for those who have been recommended to our prayers. *Pater Noster...Ave Maria....*

At the monthly intercession. Let us honour the Agonizing Heart of Jesus and the Compassionate Heart of Mary. Let us intercede for about *three millions* who are to die within a *month*, especially for those who have been recommended to our prayers. *Pater Noster. ...Ave Maria....*

At the annual intercession. Let us honour the Agonizing Heart of Jesus and the Compassionate Heart of Mary. Let us intercede for about *thirty-six millions* who are to die within *a year*, especially for those who have been recommended to our prayers. *Pater Noster...Ave Maria....*

it is therefore very important that the associates should make their intercession with this definite intention. The Directors should propose no other intentions for the intercessions, except those of the Sovereign Pontiff, of the Bishop, or some sick person. Bear in mind that those who are *dying to-day* will be *dead* to-morrow. Pray for them while there is still time to save them from hell!

PRAYER TO THE AGONIZING HEART OF JESUS.

100 days Indulgence for each recital: a Plenary Indulgence once a month. (Decret. Feb. 2, 1850.)

O clementissime Jesu, amator animarum, obsecro te per agoniam Cordis tui sanctissimi et per dolores Matris tuæ immaculatæ, lava in sanguine tuo peccatores totius mundi nunc positos in agonia et hodie morituros. Amen.

Cor Jesu in agonia factum, miserere morientium.

O most merciful Jesus, lover of souls; I pray Thee, by the agony of Thy most Sacred Heart, and by the sorrows of Thine Immaculate Mother, cleanse in Thine own Blood the sinners of the whole world who are now in their agony, and are to die this day. Amen.

Heart of Jesus in agony, pity the dying.

Note.—To gain the Plenary Indulgence, this prayer must be said at three different times each day for a month, and on the day chosen for gaining the Indulgence, it is necessary to go to Confession and Communion, and to visit a church or public oratory and there pray for the Holy Father's intentions. These Indulgences are applicable to the souls in Purgatory.

PRAYER TO THE COMPASSIONATE HEART OF MARY.

O clementissima Maria, refugium peccatorum, obsecro te per dolores cordis tui immaculati et per agoniam cordis Jesu, Filii tui dilectissimi, intercede pro peccatoribus totius mundi nunc positis in agonia et hodie morituris. Amen.

O most merciful Mary, refuge of sinners, I pray thee, by the sorrows of thy immaculate Heart, and by the agony of the Heart of Jesus, thy Beloved Son, intercede for the sinners of the whole world, who are now in their agony, and are to die this day. Amen.

Cor Mariæ compatiens, *ora pro morientibus.*

Compassionate Heart of Mary, *pray for the dying.*

Sancte Joseph, patrone bonæ mortis, *ora pro morientibus.*

Saint Joseph, Patron of a good death, *pray for the dying.*

Sancte Michael, archangele, *ora pro morientibus.*

Saint Michael, archangel, *pray for the dying.*

Sancti Angeli custodes, *orate pro morientibus.*

Holy Angel Guardians, *pray for the dying.*

Sancte Angele qui Jesum in agonia factum confortasti, *ora pro morientibus.*

Holy Angel, who didst comfort Jesus in His agony, *pray for the dying.*

THE AGONIZING HEART OF JESUS.

LITANY OF THE DYING.

Kyrie eleison. — Lord have mercy.
Christe eleison. — Christ have mercy.
Kyrie eleison. — Lord have mercy.
Sancta Maria, *ora pro eis.* — Holy Mary, *pray for them.*
Omnes sancti Angeli et Archangeli, *orate.* — All ye holy Angels and Archangels,
Sancte Abel, *ora.* — Holy Abel,
Omnis chorus justorum, *orate.* — All ye choirs of the just,
Sancte Abraham, *ora.* — Holy Abraham,
Sancte Joannes Baptista, — Saint John Baptist,
Sancte Joseph, — Saint Joseph,
Omnes Sancti Patriarchæ et Prophetæ, *orate.* — All ye holy Patriarchs and Prophets,
Sancte Petre, *ora.* — Saint Peter,
Sancte Paule, — Saint Paul,
Sancte Andrea, — Saint Andrew,
Sancte Joannes, — Saint John,
Omnes Sancti Apostoli et Evangelistæ, *orate.* — All ye holy Apostles and Evangelists,
Omnes Sancti Discipuli Domini, — All ye holy Disciples of our Lord,
Omnes Sancti Innocentes, — All ye holy Innocents,
Sancte Stephane, *ora.* — Saint Stephen,
Sancte Laurenti, — Saint Lawrence,

Pray for them.

Omnes Sancti Martyres, *orate*.	All ye holy Martyrs,
Sancte Sylvester, *ora*.	Saint Sylvester,
Sancte Gregori,	Saint Gregory,
Sancte Augustine,	Saint Augustine,
Omnes Sancti Pontifices et Confessores, *orate*.	All ye holy Bishops and Confessors,
Sancte Benedicte, *ora*.	Saint Benedict,
Sancte Francisce,	Saint Francis,
Omnes Sancti Monachi et Eremitæ, *orate*.	All ye holy Monks and Hermits,
Sancta Lucia, *ora*.	Saint Lucy,
Omnes Sanctæ Virgines et Viduæ, *orate*.	All ye holy Virgins and widows,

Pray for them.

Omnes Sancti et Sanctæ Dei, *intercedite pro eis*.	All ye men and women, Saints of God, *intercede for them*.
Propitius esto, *parce eis Domine*.	Be merciful unto them, *spare them, O Lord*.
Propitius esto, *exaudi eos, Domine*.	Be merciful unto them, *hear them, O Lord*.
Propitius esto, *libera eos, Domine*.	Be merciful unto them, *deliver them, O Lord*.
Ab ira tua, *libera eos, Domine*.	From Thy wrath, *deliver them, O Lord*.
A periculo mortis, *libera eos, Domine*.	From the dangers of eternal death, *deliver them, O Lord*.
A mala morte, *libera eos, Domine*.	From an evil death, *deliver them, O Lord*.

THE AGONIZING HEART OF JESUS. 69

A pœnis inferni, *libera eos, Domine.*
From the pains of hell, *deliver them, O Lord.*

Ab omni malo, *libera eos, Domine.*
From all evil, *deliver them, O Lord.*

A potestate diaboli,
From the power of the devil,

Per Nativitatem tuam,
By Thy Nativity,

Per crucem et Passionem tuam,
By Thy Cross and Passion,

Per mortem et sepulturam tuam,
By Thy Death and Burial,

Per gloriosam resurrectionem tuam,
By Thy glorious Resurrection,

Per admirabilem ascensionem tuam,
By Thy wonderful Ascension,

Per gratiam Spiritus Sancti Paracliti,
By the grace of the Holy Ghost, the Comforter,

Libera eos, Domine. / *Deliver them, O Lord.*

In die judicii,
In the day of Judgment,

Peccatores, *te rogamus, audi nos.*
We sinners, *beseech Thee, hear us.*

Ut eis parcas, *te rogamus, audi nos.*
That Thou spare them, *we beseech Thee hear us.*

Kyrie eleison,
Lord have mercy on them.

Christe eleison,
Christ have mercy.

Kyrie eleison,
Lord have mercy.

ACT OF REPARATION TO THE AGONIZING HEART OF JESUS.

O Jesus, who lovest souls so ardently, and who hast endured the most cruel agony to save them, behold us prostrate at Thy Feet to compassionate Thy griefs, and to make reparation to Thine Heart which is outraged daily by the sins of men! O afflicted Heart of our good Master, who can understand the terrors, the anguish, the mortal sadness which oppressed Thee in the Garden of Olives? O sweet Saviour of our souls, Thou saidst, "My soul is sorrowful even unto death," and then all our iniquities passed before Thine eyes. It was the sight of those numberless sins which wrung from Thee the doleful complaint: "Father, if it be possible, let this chalice pass from Me." But it covers us with shame and fills us with fresh grief, O Heavenly Friend of our souls, to know that we, by our own iniquities, have added to the anguish of Thine agony, and to the torments of Thy death! Oh! Jesus, pardon us! Forget our ingratitude and remember only Thine infinite mercy. Let some drops of the Divine Blood which watered the Garden of Olives, fall upon us, and upon all sinners. Let this Adorable Blood flow freely, we entreat Thee, down upon the souls of those who are now in the terrible agony of death, and about to appear at Thy dread Tribunal. O! Jesus, pity them. From the Cross Thou didst pardon the good thief; pardon the dying! Let them also hear from Thy Sacred Lips the consoling assurance, "This day thou shalt be with me in Paradise."

O! Mary, afflicted Mother, join thy supplications with our humble prayers. Unite thy homage to our expiations, and help us to repair the outrages which we have offered to the Agonizing Heart of thy Son Jesus. Blessed Archangel Michael, Angels of God, faithful guardians of our souls; Patron Saints who watch over us from Heaven, come to our aid. Lend us your holy ardour, that we may adore and love the most amiable and adorable Heart of Jesus; lend us your invincible confidence, that we may obtain from the infinite clemency of that Divine Heart, pardon for ourselves, pardon for our dear country, pardon for all sinners, pardon for the poor dying. O good Jesus, deign to receive, with this reparation, the prayers which we offer to Thee. Bless the members of this pious Association, now humbly prostrate before Thee. Kindle anew, and keep alive in their hearts, the sacred fire of Thy Divine Love, and of zeal for the salvation of souls. Above all, bless the dying. Strengthen them against the terrors of death; defend them against the attacks of the evil spirit. Open to them Thine Agonizing Heart for their refuge, and by Its Sacred Wound let them enter into the rest of a blessed Eternity. Amen.

Let us pray for the Associates and Companions, living and deceased.

Pater Noster......   Ave Maria.......

Psalm. 129.   *Psalm* 129.

De profundis clamavi ad te, Domine: Domine, exaudi vocem meam.

Out of the depths I have cried to Thee, O Lord: Lord, hear my voice.

Fiant aures tuæ intendentes in vocem deprecationis meæ.

Let Thy ears be attentive to the voice of my supplication.

Si iniquitates observaveris, Domine: Domine, quis sustinebit?

If Thou, O Lord, wilt mark iniquities, Lord, who shall stand it?

Quia apud te propitiatio est, et propter legem tuam sustinui te, Domine.

For with Thee there is merciful forgiveness: and by reason of Thy law, I have waited for Thee, O Lord.

Sustinuit anima mea in verbo ejus: speravit anima mea in Domino.

My soul hath relied on His word: my soul hath hoped in the Lord.

A custodia matutina usque ad noctem, speret Israel in Domino.

From the morning watch even until night, let Israel hope in the Lord.

Quia apud Dominum misericordia, et copiosa apud eum redemptio.

Et ipse redimet Israel, ex omnibus iniquitatibus ejus.

℣. Requiem æternam dona eis, Domine.

℟. Et lux perpetua luceat eis.

℣. Requiescant in pace.

℟. Amen.

℣. Domine exaudi orationem meam.

℟. Et clamor meus ad te veniat.

Oremus.

Fidelium, Deus, omnium conditor et redemptor, animabus famulorum famularumque tuarum remissionem cunctorum tribue peccatorum: ut indulgentiam quam semper optaverunt, piis supplicationibus consequantur. Qui vivis et

Because with the Lord there is mercy; and with Him plentiful redemption.

And He shall redeem Israel from all his iniquities.

Eternal rest give to them, O Lord.

And let perpetual light shine upon them.

May they rest in peace.

Amen.

℣. Lord, hear my prayer.

℟. And let my cry come unto Thee.

Let us pray.

O God, the Creator and Redeemer of all the faithful: grant to the souls of Thy servants departed, the remission of all their sins, that by devout supplications, they may obtain that pardon which they have always desired. Who livest

regnas, Deus, in sæcula sæculorum. ℟. Amen.

℣. Requiem æternam dona eis, Domine.

℟. Et lux perpetua luceat eis.

℣. Requiescant in pace.

℟. Amen.

and reignest world without end. Amen.

℣. Eternal rest give unto them, O Lord.

℟. And let perpetual light shine upon them.

℣. May they rest in peace.

℟. Amen.

ACT OF CONSECRATION TO THE AGONIZING HEART OF JESUS.

This may be said at the daily and monthly Intercessions, and must never be omitted at the annual one.

Adorable Jesus, Victim of love for the salvation of souls, I prostrate myself humbly before Thee; and trusting in Thy Divine mercy, I consecrate myself for ever to Thy service in this pious Association. I promise to honour, and to lead others to honour the sufferings of Thy mortal life, and, above all, Thy Holy Agony in the Garden of Olives with a special worship. I promise to promote the salvation of the dying, by my devotion and my prayers. In order to please Thee, and to save them, I offer my body and my soul, my joys and my sorrows, my life and my death, in union with Thy sufferings. O Agonizing Heart of Jesus, deign to accept this act of homage. I place it under the protection of Thine Immaculate Mother. Presented by her pure hands, may it ascend towards Thee as a sweet-smelling sacrifice, and by Thee may it reach the Throne of Thy Heavenly Father, to Whom, and to Thee, in union with the Holy Spirit, be honour and glory for ever and ever. Amen.

CHAPTER XVI.

Other Prayers and Exercises which may also be used during the time of Intercession.

DEVOTIONS TO THE AGONIZING HEART OF JESUS.

O! Jesus, my Saviour, I adore and love Thee in the mystery of Thine Agony in the Garden of Olives, and I compassionate the sufferings of Thine Agonizing Heart. I entreat Thee, by this Holy Agony, and by all the Dolours of Thy mortal life, to grant the grace of a good death to all the dying, especially to those for whom I now make intercession. For this end, let me offer Thee my most humble homage.

Agonizing Heart of Jesus, Sacred Heart of my God, my King, and my Saviour;—I adore Thee and I love Thee, have pity on the dying.

Agonizing Heart of Jesus, most holy, most chaste, most innocent of all hearts;—I adore Thee and I love Thee, have pity on the dying.

Agonizing Heart of Jesus, most humble, most submissive, most obedient of all hearts;—I adore Thee and I love Thee, have pity on the dying.

Agonizing Heart of Jesus, most afflicted, most injured, most patient of all hearts;—I adore Thee and I love Thee, have pity on the dying.

Agonizing Heart of Jesus, most sweet, most tender, most devoted of all hearts;—I adore Thee and I love Thee, have pity on the dying.

Agonizing Heart of Jesus, most generous, most noble, most powerful of all hearts;—I adore Thee and I love Thee, have pity on the dying.

Agonizing Heart of Jesus, Heart of the Good Shepherd, of the best of Friends, of the tenderest of Brothers;—I adore Thee and I love Thee, have pity on the dying.

Agonizing Heart of Jesus, Joy of the Angels, Bliss of the Saints, Glory of Heaven;—I adore Thee and I love Thee, have pity on the dying.

Agonizing Heart of Jesus, terror of demons, hope of sinners, strength and consolation of the just;—I adore Thee and I love Thee, have pity on the dying.

Agonizing Heart of Jesus, inexhaustible source of grace, abyss of mercy, only hope of the agonizing;—I adore Thee and I love Thee, have pity on the dying.

Agonizing Heart of Jesus, Beloved of the Father, Living Temple of the Holy Ghost, delight of the Immaculate Heart of Mary;—I adore Thee and I love Thee, have pity on the dying.

Agonizing Heart of Jesus, most loving, most worthy of love, most patient of all hearts;—I adore Thee and I love Thee, have pity on the dying.

Note.—These invocations may be used as Litanies, one person saying the first part and the other answering: I adore Thee and I love Thee, have pity on the dying.

ACT OF REPARATION TO THE COMPASSIONATE HEART OF MARY.

O Mary, afflicted Mother, behold us humbly prostrate at thy feet, to compassionate thy sorrows, and to make reparation for the outrages which thou receivest every day from the ungodly, and from bad christians. O most tender of mothers, who can enter into the anguish of thy most compassionate Heart, at the sight of thy dear Son Jesus, given up as a victim to the fury of His enemies! Who can understand the number and the intensity of thy sufferings, the martyrdom of thy holy soul, at the sight of this innocent Lamb, betrayed, scourged, crowned with thorns, bleeding, agonizing, expiring on the Cross!

O most afflicted of mothers, can we be insensible to thy tears and sighs! Are we not thy children? Art not thou our Mother? We compassionate thy griefs, we compassionate thy intense sorrow, and the agony of thy compassionate Heart. Our iniquities, and our ingratitude, have been the cause of thy sufferings. We come full of grief to make reparation to thee. Do not reject the sincere homage of our compassion and sorrow; thou hast suffered for us, let not so many, and such great dolours be of no avail. Present them to thy Divine Son; present His own sufferings to Him; recall to Him His sorrows, the shedding of His Blood, His Agony, His death; and entreat Him to be merciful to us. Entreat Him to shelter the Sovereign Pontiff, our Father, the Holy Church, our Mother, with His all-powerful help. Entreat Him to confound and convert their enemies. Ask of Him mercy for our dear country; mercy for the faithful of this parish and diocese; mercy for all the members of our families, and of this Association, for our benefactors, our friends and our enemies; mercy for all sinners, especially for all the dying; mercy for us all here prostrate at thy feet. Amen.

THE AGONIZING HEART OF JESUS. 79

ACT OF CONSECRATION TO THE COMPASSIONATE HEART OF MARY.

O Mary, Immaculate Virgin, Mother of God, and our Mother, desiring to honour with a special worship, the dolours of thy most compassionate Heart, I consecrate myself most humbly to thee, and lovingly offer myself to thee. I offer thee my body and my soul, my life and my death. O Queen of Martyrs, I offer thee my sufferings and my sorrows. Deign thou, in turn, to offer them to the Father in union with those of thy Divine Son, and thine own. O most compassionate Virgin, we entreat thee, by the Agonizing Heart of Jesus, thy Son, deign to take pity on the afflictions of the Holy Church, our Mother. Remember the Holy Pontiff, who has proclaimed thee Immaculate. Remember that from every end of the earth, thy children have responded to his voice, with an immense acclamation of love. It has been said, that this solemn epoch, would be to us the dawn of more peaceful days. O Immaculate Virgin, let not the expectation of thy servants and children be disappointed. Let us see these happy days. Re-kindle feeble faith and failing charity. Bring back the ages of faith, when the Holy Religion of thy Son Jesus, had the first place. O! then more than ever shalt thou be for us the Blessed Virgin. Then, more than ever, shall all generations proclaim thee Blessed. May my eyes behold the dawn of this glory, and my heart praise thee for ever. Amen.

SUPPLICATION TO THE COMPASSIONATE HEART OF MARY.

O Queen of Martyrs! who hast, in every age, overthrown heresies, stretch forth the arm of thy power against the spirit of Satan, now unchained upon earth, and against the men of sin, who have become his agents. Behold the impious war which they do not cease to wage against Jesus Christ, thy Son, His Vicar, His Church, His Bishops, His Priests, and His Children. See, the ruins which they have heaped around us, the waves of blood which they have caused to flow, the countless souls which they have perverted, and cast into hell. O! Holy Virgin, powerful Help of Christians, we entreat thee, come to our aid. Come quickly with the celestial army, especially the intrepid Archangel Michael. Kindle in all hearts, especially in the hearts of Priests, the sacred fire of most ardent zeal. Place thyself at our head, august Mother of the God of hosts, and lead us to the battle. Sustain us by thy prayers; encourage us by thine eye. Scatter before us these new infernal legions, as the wind scatters the clouds. Powerful Help of Christians, give us victory, give us triumph and peace; obtain for us a holy life and a holy death. Amen.

Who is like to God, quis ut Deus? Who is like to Jesus, Son of God and of Mary, quis ut Jesus? Amen.

OFFERING OF OUR OWN LIFE FOR THE AGONIZING.

Eternal and all-powerful God, though I am most unworthy to appear before Thee, nevertheless, trusting in Thine infinite goodness, I offer myself most humbly as a victim to Thy Divine Majesty, in honour of, and in union with, the Agonizing Heart of Thy Beloved Son Jesus. Dispose of my life, of my prayers, and of my sufferings, according to Thy good pleasure, for the salvation of all the dying, especially the dying of this day. Amen.

PRAYER TO ST. JOSEPH, THE PATRON OF A GOOD DEATH.

O most merciful Joseph, patron of a good death, I beseech thee, by the Agonizing Heart of Jesus, and by the compassionate Heart of Mary, thine Immaculate Spouse, intercede for all the sinners in the world, who are now in their agony, and who are to die this day. Amen.

Saint Joseph, patron of a good death, pray for the dying.

PRAYER TO THE GUARDIAN ANGELS OF THE DYING.

O Sancti Angeli, obsecro vos per Cor Jesu in agoniâ factum et per Cor compatiens Mariæ, Reginæ vestræ immaculatæ, intercedite pro morientibus custodiæ vestræ commissis; servate eos à malo, confirmate eos in bono, liberate eos ab insidiis diaboli, ut per vos mortem sanctam adepti, per vos feliciter in sanctorum consortium deducantur. Amen.

O holy Angels, I beseech you, by the Agonizing Heart of Jesus, and by the compassionate Heart of Mary, your Immaculate Queen, intercede for the dying confided to your care, preserve them from evil, confirm them in good, deliver them from the snares of the devil, that, having through your aid obtained the grace of a good death, they may, by you, be brought with joy into the company of the Saints. Amen.

Sancti Angeli custodes, *orate pro morientibus.*

Sancte Michael archangele, *ora pro morientibus.*

Sancte Angele qui Jesum in agoniâ factum confortasti, *ora pro morientibus.*

Holy guardian Angels, *pray for the dying.*

Holy Archangel, Saint Michael, *pray for the dying.*

Holy Angel, who strengthened Jesus in His Agony, *pray for the dying.*

INVOCATION OF JESUS, MARY, AND JOSEPH.

Jesus, Mary, and Joseph, I offer you my heart and my soul.

Jesus, Mary, and Joseph, assist me in my last agony.

Jesus, Mary, and Joseph, may I breathe forth my soul with you in peace.

Pius VII., by a decree of 28th April, 1807, granted for ever an indulgence of 300 days to the faithful, each time they say devoutly, and with a contrite heart, these three ejaculations; and if only one of them is said, an indulgence of 100 days,—all applicable to the souls in Purgatory.

THREE PATERS AND AVES FOR THE FAITHFUL IN THEIR AGONY.

The three "Pater Nosters" are said in memory of the Agony of our Lord Jesus Christ, and the three "Ave Marias" in memory of the dolours of the Blessed Virgin Mary. These prayers should be said kneeling, unless in case of indisposition.

I. An Indulgence of 300 days to all Christians, every time that, praying for the faithful in their agony, they shall say, with contrite heart and with devotion, three *Pater Nosters* in remembrance of the Passion and Agony of Jesus Christ, and three *Ave Marias* in memory of the bitter sorrow undergone by most holy Mary, whilst assisting at the Agony of her beloved Son Jesus.

II. A Plenary Indulgence, and remission of all sins, to those who shall practise this pious exercise once a day, at least, for an entire month; to be gained on any one day in the month, when, after Confession and Communion, they shall pray according to the mind of the Sovereign Pontiff. (Pius VII. 18th April, 1809.)

PERPETUAL INTERCESSION TO

EJACULATORY PRAYER, OR OFFERING OF THE PRECIOUS BLOOD OF OUR LORD JESUS CHRIST.

Eternal Father! I offer Thee the Precious Blood of Jesus, in satisfaction for my sins, and for the wants of Holy Church.

The Indulgence of 100 days to all the faithful, each time they say this ejaculation. (Granted by Pope Pius VII. in a rescript, signed with his own hand, March 22, 1817.)

TO MARY.

Ave Maria doloribus plena: crucifixus tecum: lacrymabilis tu in mulieribus, et lacrymabilis fructus ventris tui Jesus. Sancta Maria, Mater crucifixi, lacrymas impertire nobis crucifixoribus Filii tui, nunc et in hora mortis nostræ. Amen.

Hail Mary, full of sorrows, the Crucified is with thee, tearful art thou amongst women, and worthy of tears is the fruit of thy womb, Jesus. Holy Mary, Mother of the Crucified, obtain tears for us crucifiers of thy Son, now, and at the hour of our death. Amen.

His Holiness Pope Pius IX. (by decree of Dec. 23rd, 1847,) granted 100 days Indulgence to all the faithful, every time they say this prayer with a contrite heart.

My Jesus mercy!

(100 days Indulgence each time.)

Sweet Heart of Mary, be my salvation.

(300 days Indulgence each time.)

PRAYER TO ST. MICHAEL THE ARCHANGEL FOR THE DYING.

Hail, most glorious Saint Michael! hail most merciful leader of the Heavenly host! hail, honour and glory of the Angelic hierarchy! O most illustrious Prince, O sublime hero, ornament of Paradise, brilliant jewel of the Celestial Palace; full of wisdom, perfect in beauty, thou art the impress of the Divine likeness; gold and precious stones increase thy splendour; thou dost walk in the fulness of joy through Paradise; thou dost proceed to the mount of God, through the midst of shining fires; thou hast been appointed by God, the Prince of souls, thou dost raise them up, and bring them into the dwelling of eternal joy. I venture, blessed Prince, to remind thee of all the graces, which the infinite bounty of God has bestowed upon thee, above all orders of Angels; and I pray thee, by the mutual love of the three Divine Persons, deign to receive my soul at my last hour, and to gain favour for me from the Divine Judge, by the power of thy intercession. Grant the same protection to all the dying, for whom I now intercede, and obtain for them the grace of a holy death. Amen.

PRAYER TO THE ANGEL WHO STRENGTHENED JESUS IN HIS AGONY IN THE GARDEN OF OLIVES.

O holy Angel, who didst strengthen Jesus, during His Agony in the Garden of Olives, deign to strengthen those who are now in their agony, for whom I intercede. Make intercession for them. Obtain for them courage to resist the assaults of the devil, to bear their sufferings with patience, to make the sacrifice of their life to God with love. Beg their angel-guardians, their holy Patrons, and all the Heavenly host, to ask these graces for them, and to come to their aid. Above all, entreat the Queen of Angels, the august Mother of God, to surround them with her powerful protection, to be their advocate with her Divine Son Jesus, to gain mercy for them, and the grace of a holy death. Amen.

ANOTHER PRAYER TO THE GUARDIAN ANGELS OF THE DYING.

Holy Angels, guardians of those in their agony, now about to appear at God's tribunal, kindly watch over them with the greatest care. Do not let these souls committed to you, be lost for ever. Beseech Jesus, their most merciful Saviour, that the merits of His Agony and death, may not be in vain for them. Entreat Mary, their tender Mother, to remember that her beloved Son Jesus, sweated blood in the Garden of Olives, and endured death on Calvary to save them. Ask their holy Patrons, and all the inhabitants of the Heavenly courts, to pray for them, to the Agonizing Heart of Jesus, and, O holy guardian-angels, until their last breath is drawn, let your prayers and entreaties urge the loving Saviour, in His infinite mercy to pardon them, and bring them into His Eternal Kingdom. Amen.

PRAYER TO ST. JOHN THE EVANGELIST FOR THE DYING.

Great Saint, who wast present at the Agony of Jesus, in the Garden of Olives, and upon the Cross, be present also at the agony of His members. Give this charitable assistance to all the dying, for whom I intercede this day, especially to those who have been recommended to our prayers. Intercede for them, and obtain for them, the grace of a holy death. O! beloved disciple of Jesus, ask the same favour for us, and for all dear to us. At the hour of our agony, be near us and protect us. Prepare us by a holy life, and by the imitation of thy virtues, for that great moment which shall decide our eternal destiny. Above all, obtain for us, a tender and real devotion to the Agonizing Heart of Jesus, and to the compassionate Heart of Mary, so that, having honoured them on earth, we may love and praise them eternally with thee in Heaven. Amen.

INVOCATIONS.

Holy Mary Magdalen, model of love and of penance, who didst stand at the foot of the Cross, during the agony and death of Jesus Christ, pray for the dying,

O good thief, who, at the point of death, didst hear from the lips of Jesus, the consoling words: "This day shalt thou be with Me in Paradise," pray for the dying.

Saint Mary Magdalen of Pazzi, angel, by thine innocence, seraph, by thy love, martyr, by thy mortification, apostle, by thy zeal for souls, pray for the dying.

PRAISES TO OUR LORD, BY ST. GERTRUDE.
(Offer them for the dying, to the Agonizing Heart of Jesus.)

Hail, life-giving germ of Divine Majesty! hail, unfading Flower of human dignity; O most loving Jesus, for all the blasphemies and contumely with which Thou wast assailed on earth, I salute and bless Thee, with all the affection and love of the whole creation.

For every drop of Thy most Precious Blood shed in Thy Passion, for every wound Thou didst bear in Thy Sacred Body, for every blow, and stripe, and bruise, I salute and bless Thee ten thousandfold.

For every tear Thou didst shed, for every sigh Thou didst breathe forth, for every sorrow Thou didst feel, I bless and salute Thee, O my sweetest Jesus, ten thousandfold.

For every act of virtue Thou didst do, for every thirsting desire with which Thou didst yearn for our salvation, for every look of love Thou didst bend on Thy Mother and Thy friends, I bless and salute Thee ten thousandfold.

For every fall along Thy way of sorrows, for every shrinking and sinking of Thy human Flesh, for every movement of Thy sacred Hands and Feet, I salute and bless Thee ten thousandfold.

I bless and salute Thee ten thousand times, O meekest Jesus, for every drop of blood that fell to the ground in Thy sweat of Agony, for every painful step of Thy weary Feet, for every strong cry and tear, wherewith Thou didst offer Thy prayers and Thy supplications to Thy Father.

I salute and bless Thee ten thousand times, O most gentle Jesus, for every gash wherewith Thy Sacred Body was torn in Thy scourging, for every thorn of Thy cruel crown, which entered into Thy Flesh, for all the loathsome spitting, with which Thou wast defiled.

I bless and salute Thee ten thousand times, for every cord with which Thou wast bound, for every reproach and outrage wherewith Thy Soul was saturated, for every impious greeting of scorn with which Thou wast insulted.

For every false charge brought against Thee, O sinless Jesus, for every foul and impious lie uttered in disparagement of Thee, and for every unjust sentence pronounced upon Thee, I bless and salute Thee ten thousandfold.

Would, O most gracious Jesus, that I could multiply these, my salutations and praises, ten thousand times ten thousandfold, and offer them to Thee every hour of my life; that so I might efface, and make amends for, all the insults, the contumely, and the blasphemy hurled against Thee, my sweetest Redeemer! I pray Thee, despise not the desire nor the sighing of Thy poor, but, according to Thine own essential goodness, deign to ratify and accept them. Amen.—(St. Gertrude, Book 4, chap. 22.)

LITANY OF THE SACRED HEART OF JESUS.

Kyrie eleison.	Lord have mercy.
Christe eleison.	Christ have mercy.
Kyrie eleison.	Lord have mercy.
Christe audi nos.	Christ hear us.
Christe exaudi nos.	Christ graciously hear us.
Pater de cœlis, Deus, *miserere nobis.*	God, the Father of Heaven, *have mercy on us.*

THE AGONIZING HEART OF JESUS.

Fili, Redemptor mundi Deus, *miserere nobis.*	God the Son, Redeemer of the world, *have mercy on us.*
Spiritus Sancte, Deus,	God, the Holy Ghost,
Sancta Trinitas, unus Deus,	Holy Trinity, one God,
Cor Jesu, Verbo Dei substantialiter unitum,	Heart of Jesus, hypostatically united with the Word of God,
Cor Jesu, Divinitatis sanctuarium,	Heart of Jesus, Sanctuary of the Divinity,
Cor Jesu, Sanctæ Trinitatis templum,	Heart of Jesus, Temple of the Holy Trinity,
Cor Jesu, sapientiæ abyssus,	Heart of Jesus, abyss of wisdom,
Cor Jesu, bonitatis oceanus,	Heart of Jesus, ocean of goodness,
Cor Jesu, misericordiæ thronus,	Heart of Jesus, Throne of mercy,
Cor Jesu, thesaurus nunquam deficiens,	Heart of Jesus, Treasure inexhaustible,
Cor Jesu, de cujus plenitudine omnes nos accepimus,	Heart of Jesus, of Whose fulness we have all received,
Cor Jesu, pax et reconciliatio nostra,	Heart of Jesus, our Peace and our atonement,
Cor Jesu, virtutum omnium exemplar,	Heart of Jesus, model of all virtues,

Miserere nobis. / *Have mercy on us.*

Cor Jesu, infinite amans et infinite amandum, *miserere nobis.*

Cor Jesu, fons aquæ salientis in vitam æternam,

Cor Jesu, in quo sibi Pater bene complacuit,

Cor Jesu, propitiatio pro peccatis nostris,

Cor Jesu, propter nos amaritudine repletum,

Cor Jesu, usque ad mortem in Horto tristissimum,

Cor Jesu, opprobriis saturatum,

Cor Jesu, amore vulneratum,

Cor Jesu, lancea perforatum,

Cor Jesu, in cruce sanguine exhaustum,

Heart of Jesus, infinitely loving, and infinitely worthy of being loved, *have mercy on us.*

Heart of Jesus, Fountain of water springing up into everlasting life,

Heart of Jesus, in which the Father is well-pleased,

Heart of Jesus, the propitiation for our sins,

Heart of Jesus, filled with bitterness for our sakes,

Heart of Jesus, sorrowful in the Garden even unto death,

Heart of Jesus, saturated with revilings,

Heart of Jesus, wounded with love,

Heart of Jesus, pierced with a lance,

Heart of Jesus, exhausted of Thy Blood upon the Cross,

Miserere nobis.

Have mercy on us.

THE AGONIZING HEART OF JESUS. 93

Cor Jesu, attritum propter scelera nostra, *miserere nobis.*

Cor Jesu, etiam nunc ab ingratis hominibus, in SS. amoris Sacramento dilaceratum,

Cor Jesu, refugium peccatorum,

Cor Jesu, fortitudo debilium,

Cor Jesu, consolatio afflictorum,

Cor Jesu, perseverantia justorum,

Cor Jesu, salus in te sperantium,

Cor Jesu, spes in te morientium,

Cor Jesu, cultorum tuorum dulce præsidium,

Cor Jesu, deliciæ Sanctorum omnium,

Cor Jesu, adjutor in tribulationibus quæ invenerunt nos nimis,

Miserere nobis.

Heart of Jesus, bruised for our sins, *have mercy on us.*

Heart of Jesus, still outraged by ungrateful men in the most holy Sacrament of love,

Heart of Jesus, refuge of sinners,

Heart of Jesus, strength of the weak,

Heart of Jesus, comfort of the afflicted,

Heart of Jesus, perseverance of the just,

Heart of Jesus, salvation of them that hope in Thee,

Heart of Jesus, hope of them that die in Thee,

Heart of Jesus, sweet support of those who worship Thee,

Heart of Jesus, delight of all the Saints,

Heart of Jesus, our helper in our many and great tribulations,

Have mercy on us.

Agnus Dei, qui tollis peccata mundi,	Lamb of God, who takest away the sins of the world, *spare us, O Jesus*.
Agnus Dei, qui tollis peccata mundi,	Lamb of God, who takest away the sins of the world, *Hear us, O Jesus*.
Agnus Dei, qui tollis, peccata mundi,	Lamb of God, who takest away the sins of the world, *Have mercy on us, O Jesus*.
Christe audi nos,	Christ hear us.
Christe exaudi nos.	Christ graciously hear us.

Oremus.

Omnipotens sempiterne Deus, respice in Cor dilectissimi Filii tui, et in laudes et satisfactiones quas in nomine peccatorum tibi persolvit, atque misericordiam tuam petentibus tu veniam concede placatus, in nomine ejusdem Jesu Christi Filii tui, qui tecum vivit et regnat in sæcula sæculorum. Amen.

LITANY OF THE BLESSED VIRGIN.

Kyrie eleison,
Christe eleison.
Kyrie eleison.
Christe audi nos.
Christe exaudi nos.
Pater de cœlis, Deus, *miserere nobis.*
Fili Redemptor mundi, Deus, *miserere nobis.*
Spiritus Sancte Deus, *miserere nobis.*
Sancta Trinitas, unus Deus, *miserere nobis.*
Sancta Maria, *ora pro nobis.*
Sancta Dei Genitrix,
Sancta Virgo Virginum,
Mater Christi,
Mater Divinæ gratiæ,
Mater purissima,
Mater castissima,
Mater inviolata,
Mater intemerata,
Mater amabilis,
Mater admirabilis,
Mater Creatoris,
Mater Salvatoris,
Virgo prudentissima, *Ora pro nobis.*

Virgo veneranda,
Virgo prædicanda,
Virgo potens,
Virgo clemens,
Virgo fidelis,
Speculum justitiæ,
Sedes sapientiæ,
Causa nostræ lætitiæ,
Vas spirituale,
Vas honorabile,
Vas insigne devotionis,
Rosa mystica,
Turris Davidica,
Turris eburnea,
Domus aurea,
Fœderis arca,
Janua cœli,
Stella matutina,
Salus infirmorum,
Refugium peccatorum,
Consolatrix afflictorum,
Auxilium Christianorum,
Regina Angelorum,
Regina Patriarcharum,
Regina Prophetarum,
Regina Apostolorum,
Regina Martyrum, *Ora pro nobis.*

Regina confessorum, *ora pro nobis.*
Regina Virginum, *ora pro nobis.*
Regina Sanctorum omnium, *ora pro nobis.*
Regina sine labe originali concepta, *ora pro nobis.*
Agnus Dei, qui tollis peccata mundi, *parce nobis Domine.*
Agnus Dei, qui tollis peccata mundi, *exaudi nos Domine.*
Agnus Dei, qui tollis peccata mundi, *miserere nobis.*
Christe audi nos.
Christe exaudi nos.
℣. Ora pro nobis, sancta Dei Genitrix.
℞. Ut digni efficiamur promissionibus Christi.

Oremus.

Gratiam tuam, quæsumus, Domine, mentibus nostris infunde, ut qui, Angelo nuntiante, Christi Filii tui Incarnationem cognovimus, per Passionem ejus et crucem ad Resurrectionis gloriam perducamur. Per eumdem Christum Dominum nostrum. ℞. Amen.

INVOCATIONS BY ST. IGNATIUS. ANIMA CHRISTI.

His Holiness, Pope Pius IX. revoking all other Indulgences attached to these invocations, has granted : 1st, an Indulgence of 300 days, to all the faithful every time they shall say them with a contrite heart. 2nd, an Indulgence of seven years and seven quarantines to all Priests who shall say them after Mass, or faithful, who shall say them after Communion. 3rd, a Plenary Indulgence once a month, to all those who have the good custom of saying them, at least, once a day: to be gained on that day, when after Confession and Communion, they shall visit some church or public oratory, and pray there for some time, according to the intention of his Holiness. (Decree of Jan. 9, 1854.)

Anima Christi, sanctifica me.	Soul of Christ, sanctify me.
Corpus Christi, salva me.	Body of Christ, save me.
Sanguis Christi, inebria me.	Blood of Christ, inebriate me.
Aqua lateris Christi, lava me.	Water from the side of Christ, wash me.
Passio Christi, conforta me.	Passion of Christ, strengthen me.
O bone Jesu, exaudi me.	O good Jesus, hear me.
Intra tua vulnera absconde me.	In Thy wounds, hide me.
Ne permittas me separari a Te.	Suffer me not to be separated from Thee.
Ab hoste maligno defende me.	From the malignant enemy defend me.
In hora mortis meæ voca me,	In the hour of my death call me,
Et jube me venire ad Te;	And bid me come unto Thee;
Ut cum Sanctis tuis laudem Te,	That with Thy Saints I may praise Thee
In sæcula, sæculorum. Amen.	For all eternity Amen.

ANOTHER PRAYER OF ST. IGNATIUS.

Suscipe, Domine, universam meam libertatem. Accipe memoriam, intellectum, atque voluntatem omnem. Quidquid habeo, vel possideo, tu mihi largitus es; id tibi totum restituo, ac tuæ prorsus voluntati trado gubernandum. Amorem tui solum cum gratia tua mihi dones, et dives sum satis, nec aliud quidquam ultra posco.

Take, O Lord, all my liberty, my memory, my understanding, and my whole will. Whatever I have or possess, Thou hast bestowed on me. I restore the whole to Thee, and hand it over entirely to Thy will to be governed. Grant me Thy love alone with Thy grace, and I am sufficiently rich; nor do I ask for anything besides.

INVOCATIONS.

St. Michael, archangel, *pray for the dying.*
St. Gabriel and St. Raphael,
All ye blessed spirits,
St. John the Baptist,
St. Peter and St. Paul,
St. Joachim and St. Anne,
St. Lazarus and St. Martha,
St. Basil and St. Gregory,
St. Augustine and St. Monica,
St. Antony and St. Paul,

St. Jerome and St. Bernard, *pray for the dying.*
St. Leonard and St. Genoveva,
St. Benedict and St. Scholastica,
St. Dominic and St. Vincent Ferrer,
St. Francis of Assisi and St. Clare,
St. Thomas of Aquin and St. Bonaventure,
St. Ignatius and St. Francis Xavier,
St. Catherine of Sienna and St. Theresa,
St. Rose of Lima and St. Colette,
St. Francis of Sales and St. Chantal,
St. Vincent de Paul and St. Joseph de Cupertino,
St. Antony of Padua and St. Bernardine of Sienna,
St. Camillus of Lellis and St. Philip Neri,
St. John of the Cross and St. Peter of Alcantara,
St. Louis of Gonzaga and St. Stanislaus Kostka,
All ye Saints,

PRAYER TO JESUS AGONIZING IN HONOUR OF HIS SWEAT OF BLOOD IN THE GARDEN OF OLIVES.

Remember, O my Divine Saviour, Thine anguish and fear, when being in an agony, Thou didst prolong Thy prayer; and Martyr to suffering, desire, and love, didst water the ground with a sweat of blood. O tender Lamb, let me, with the deepest reverence and love, gather up each drop of Thy Precious Blood, and offer them all to Thee for my salvation and that of the dying. Deign to apply Its merits to us, and having purified us by Its virtue from all our stains, bring us to the dwelling of eternal joy. Amen.

PRAYER TO JESUS IN AGONY ON THE CROSS.

O my beloved Jesus, on the Cross for love of me, enduring with infinite patience sufferings upon sufferings, not only bodily pains, but the most grievous affliction of soul, in being forsaken by Thy Heavenly Father; have compassion on all who are in their agony, and upon me, when I shall be in this extremity. And grant us, by the merits of Thy Precious Blood, grace to bear all the pains and anguish of our agony with true patience, so that, uniting our sufferings to Thine, we may be made partakers of Thy glory in Heaven. Amen.

PRAYER TO MARY STANDING AT THE FOOT OF THE CROSS.

O! Mary, glorious and Blessed Virgin, who didst die consumed by the ardour of divine love; to whom death was a sweet sleep, soon ended by thine awakening to immortality, pray for us sinners, now and at the hour of our death. Do not forsake thy poor children at that awful moment. Thou, who didst stand at the foot of the Cross of thy dying Son, come to

receive the last sighs of those who now invoke
thee with entire confidence. Remember that
if death was a triumph to thee, it is a chastisement to us. Have mercy on all afflicted souls,
who call on thee as their Mother and their
hope. Pray for us all, assist us all. Obtain
for us grace to bear our sufferings with
resignation, and to make the sacrifice of our
life cheerfully to God. In preparation for the
hour of death, we unite ourselves beforehand
to the holy dispositions of thy compassionate
Heart, and of the Agonizing Heart of thy
Divine Son Jesus in the Garden of Olives, and
upon the Cross. Sanctify our sufferings,
sanctify our agony. Let thy maternal protection be extended even to those poor souls who
know thee not, who outrage thy Beloved Son,
who persevere in refusing the offers of His
mercy and of His love. Obtain for them the
powerful grace of conversion which breaks and
transforms the heart, and of the most hardened
sinners often makes the greatest saints. Amen.

ANOTHER PRAYER TO MARY, MOTHER OF SORROWS.

O most sorrowful Mother, by the cruel
martyrdom which thou didst suffer at the foot
of the Cross, during the three hours of the
Agony of thy beloved Son Jesus, assist us in
our agony, for we are the children of thy

sorrows, and intercede for us that we may pass from our deathbed to join the blessed, who are ever with thee in heaven. Amen.

RECOMMENDATION TO ST. JOSEPH, THE PATRON OF A GOOD DEATH.

O glorious St. Joseph, who in thine agony, and at the moment of thy death, didst enjoy the presence of Jesus and Mary, obtain the same blessing for the dying for whom I now intercede, particularly for those who have been recommended to my prayers. I ask this grace also for myself, and for those belonging to me, when we shall be in our agony. In that hour remember us, O great Saint! and by thy powerful protection, obtain for us the grace of a peaceful death like thine, in the arms of Jesus and Mary. Amen.

RECOMMENDATION TO ST. MICHAEL THE ARCHANGEL PROTECTOR OF SOULS.

Glorious Archangel Michael, who didst fight with such courage against the army of the rebellious angels, hasten to the help of the dying. See with what fury the devil haunts their bed to devour them. See with what perfidy he strives to hold them fast in the bonds of sin, to harden them, and to cast them into hell. O charitable protector of souls, hasten to help the dying. Excite in their hearts sentiments of lively faith and sincere penitence; give them fresh confidence; re-kindle the sacred fire of divine love; alleviate their sufferings; obtain for them resignation; defend them in their agony. Lastly, after having helped them to gain the victory, lead them to the dwelling of the elect. Amen.

Psalm 50. *Miserere.*

1 Have mercy on me, O God: according to Thy great mercy.

2 And according to the multitude of Thy tender mercies: blot out my iniquity.

3 Wash me yet more from my iniquity: and cleanse me from my sin.

4 For I know my iniquity: and my sin is always before me.

5 To Thee only have I sinned, and have done evil before Thee: that Thou mayest be justified in Thy words, and mayest overcome when Thou art judged.

6 For behold, I was conceived in iniquities: and in sins did my mother conceive me.

7 For behold, Thou hast loved truth: the uncertain and hidden things of Thy wisdom Thou hast made manifest to me.

8 Thou shalt sprinkle me with hyssop, and I shall be cleansed: Thou shalt wash me, and I shall be made whiter than snow.

9 To my hearing Thou shalt give joy and

gladness: and the bones that have been humbled shall rejoice.

10 Turn away Thy face from my sins: and blot out all my iniquities.

11 Create a clean heart in me, O God: and renew a right spirit within my bowels.

12 Cast me not away from Thy face: and take not Thy Holy Spirit from me.

13 Restore unto me the joy of Thy salvation: and strengthen me with a perfect spirit.

14 I will teach the unjust Thy ways: and the wicked shall be converted to Thee.

15 Deliver me from blood, O God, Thou God of my salvation: and my tongue shall extol Thy justice.

16 O Lord, Thou wilt open my lips: and my mouth shall declare Thy praise.

17 For if Thou hadst desired sacrifice, I would indeed have given it: with burnt offerings Thou wilt not be delighted.

18 A sacrifice to God is an afflicted spirit; a contrite and humble heart, O God, Thou wilt not despise.

19 Deal favourably, O Lord, in Thy good will with Sion: that the walls of Jerusalem may be built up.

20 Then shalt Thou accept the sacrifice of justice, oblations, and whole burnt-offerings: then shall they lay calves upon Thine altar.

Glory be to the Father, and to the Son, and to the Holy Ghost:

As it was in the beginning, is now, and ever shall be, world without end. Amen.

Spare Thy people, O Lord, spare Thy people, and be not angry with us for ever.

Spare Thy people, O Lord, spare Thy people, and be not angry with us for ever.

Spare Thy people, O Lord, spare Thy people, and be not angry with us for ever.

AT BENEDICTION OF THE MOST HOLY SACRAMENT.

O Salutaris Hostia.

O saving Victim opening wide
   The gate of heav'n to man below!
Our foes press on from every side:
   Thine aid supply, Thy strength bestow.

To Thy great name be endless praise,
   Immortal Godhead, one in Three!
Oh, grant us endless length of days
   In our true native land with Thee. Amen.

Tantum ergo Sacramentum.

Down in adoration falling,
   Lo! the sacred Host we hail;
Lo! o'er ancient forms departing,
   Newer rites of grace prevail;
Faith for all defects supplying
   Where the feeble senses fail.

To the everlasting Father,
  And the Son who reigns on high,
With the Holy Ghost proceeding
  Forth from each eternally,
Be salvation, honour, blessing,
  Might, and endless majesty!

℣. Thou didst give them bread from heaven.
℟. Containing in itself all sweetness.

Let us pray.

O God, who, under a wonderful Sacrament, hast left us a memorial of Thy passion; grant us, we beseech Thee, so to venerate the sacred mysteries of Thy Body and Blood, that we may ever feel within us the fruit of Thy redemption. Who livest, &c. Amen.

PROSE TO THE BLESSED SACRAMENT.

Hail to Thee! true Body, sprung
From the Virgin Mary's womb!
The same that on the Cross was hung,
And bore for man the bitter doom!
Thou, whose side was pierc'd and flow'd,
Both with water and with blood:
Suffer us to taste of Thee,
In our life's last agony.
O kind, O loving One!
O sweet Jesu, Mary's Son!

HYMN TO THE HOLY SPIRIT.

Come, O Creator Spirit blest!
And in our souls take up Thy rest:
Come, with Thy grace and heavenly aid,
To fill the hearts which Thou hast made.

Great Paraclete! to Thee we cry;
O highest gift of God most high!
O fount of life! O fire of love!
And sweet anointing from above!

Thou in Thy sevenfold gifts art known;
The finger of God's hand we own;
The promise of the Father Thou!
Who dost the tongue with pow'r endow.

Kindle our senses from above,
And make our hearts o'erflow with love:
With patience firm, and virtue high,
The weakness of our flesh supply.

Far from us drive the foe we dread,
And grant us Thy true peace instead;
So shall we not, with Thee for guide,
Turn from the path of life aside.

Oh, may Thy grace on us bestow,
The Father and the Son to know,
And Thee through endless times confess'd
Of both th' eternal Spirit blest.

All glory while the ages run
Be to the Father, and the Son

Who rose from death; the same to Thee,
O Holy Ghost, eternally. Amen.

℣. Send forth Thy Spirit, and they shall be created.

℟. And Thou shalt renew the face of the earth.

Let us pray.

O God, who hast taught the hearts of the faithful by the light of Thy Holy Spirit, grant us, by the same Spirit, to have a right judgment in all things, and evermore to rejoice in His consolation. Through Christ our Lord. Amen.

HYMN TO THE SACRED HEART OF JESUS.

Hail Victim of surpassing love,
   Best hope of mortals here below;
   Our only solace in our woe
Eternal joy of Heaven above!

Thou art the Godhead's glory bright,
   Thou art in God the Son's pure breast,
   The Holy Ghost in Thee doth rest,
The Father finds in Thee delight.

The sun is dark compared to Thee,
   Thou art a palace and a shrine
   For the eternal Word Divine,
More worthy than the heavens can be.

THE AGONIZING HEART OF JESUS.

The Holy Ghost in solemn hour,
   O'ershadowing the Virgin blest,
   Form'd Thee within her spotless breast,
By miracle of love and pow'r.

O sweetest Heart, most loving Heart,
   Thy love for man hath wounded Thee,
   Now in Thy mercy grant to me
Of that surpassing love a part.

Our sins are great, our sins are sore,
   And they have angered God on high,
   But when He turns on Thee His eye
He can remember them no more.

And by the cruel soldier's spear
   That made a wound so deep and great,
   Thy love has opened wide a gate
And bids us enter without fear.

Since Thou dost love our souls so well
   That Thou hast given from all Thy veins,
   Thy Blood to wash us from our stains,
Let us for ever in Thee dwell.

O Jesu! Son of God above,
   Of holy souls the Friend Divine,
   Our hearts and all we have are Thine,
Reign ever over all by love!

HYMN TO THE BLESSED VIRGIN MARY.

Hail, thou star of ocean!
  Portal of the sky!
Ever Virgin Mother
  Of the Lord most high!

Oh! by Gabriel's ave
  Utter'd long ago,
Eva's name reversing,
  'Stablish peace below.

Break the captive's fetters;
  Light on blindness pour;
All our ills expelling,
  Every bliss implore.

Shew thyself a mother;
  Offer Him our sighs,
Who for us incarnate
  Did not thee despise.

Virgin of all virgins!
  To thy shelter take us;
Gentlest of the gentle!
  Chaste and gentle make us.

Still as on we journey,
  Help our weak endeavour;
Till with thee and Jesus
  We rejoice for ever.

THE AGONIZING HEART OF JESUS.

Through the highest heaven,
   To the Almighty Three,
Father, Son and Spirit,
   One same glory be. Amen.

℣. Pray for us most holy Virgin,

℟. That we may be made worthy of the promises of Christ.

Grant, O merciful God, support to our frailty; that we, who commemorate the holy Mother of God, may, by the help of her intercession, arise from our iniquities. Through the same Christ our Lord, &c.

We fly to thy patronage, O holy Mother of God, despise not our petitions in our necessities; but deliver us always from all dangers, O glorious and blessed Virgin.

Mary, conceived without sin, pray for us, who trust in thee.

Praised be the Agonizing Heart of Jesus!

Praised be the compassionate Heart of Mary!

THE HYMN "STABAT MATER."

At the Cross her station keeping
Stood the mournful Mother weeping,
   Close to Jesus to the last:

Through her heart, His sorrow sharing,
All His bitter anguish bearing,
   Now at length the sword had passed.

O how sad and sore distress'd
Was that Mother, highly blest,
 Of the sole-begotten One!

Christ above in torment hangs;
She beneath beholds the pangs,
 Of her dying glorious Son.

Is there one who would not weep,
'Whelmed in miseries so deep,
 Christ's dear Mother to behold?

Can the human heart refrain
From partaking in her pain,
 In that Mother's pain untold?

Bruised, derided, cursed, defiled,
She beheld her tender Child,
 All with bloody scourges rent;

For the sins of His own nation
Saw Him hang in desolation
 Till His Spirit forth He sent.

O thou Mother! fount of love!
Touch my spirit from above,
 Make my heart with thine accord:

Make me feel as thou hast felt;
Make my soul to glow and melt
 With the love of Christ my Lord.

Holy Mother! pierce me through;
In my heart each wound renew
  Of my Saviour crucified;
Let me share with thee His pain,
Who for all my sins was slain,
  Who for me in torment died.

Let me mingle tears with thee,
Mourning Him who mourned for me,
  All the days that I may live:
By the Cross with thee to stay;
There with thee to weep and pray,
  Is all I ask of thee to give.

Virgin of all virgins blest!
Listen to my fond request:
  Let me share thy grief divine;
Let me to my latest breath,
In my body bear the death,
  Of that dying Son of thine.

Wounded with His every wound,
Steep my soul till it hath swooned
  In His very blood away;
Be to me, O Virgin, nigh,
Lest in flames I burn and die
  In His awful judgment day.

Christ when Thou shalt call me hence,
Be Thy Mother my defence,
  Be Thy Cross my victory:

While my body here decays,
May my soul Thy goodness praise
 Safe in Paradise with Thee. Amen.

PRAYER OF ST. BERNARD TO THE BLESSED VIRGIN.

(300 days indulgence for each recital. Plenary Indulgence once a month on the usual conditions, to those who say it every day.)

Memorare, O piissima Virgo Maria, non esse auditum a sæculo quemquam ad tua currentem præsidia tua implorantem auxilia, tua petentem suffragia, esse derelictum: ego, tali animatus confidentia, ad te Virgo virginum, Mater, curro, ad te, venio; coram te gemens peccator assisto; noli, Mater Verbi verba mea despicere, sed audi propitia et exaudi. Amen.

Remember, O most gracious Virgin Mary, that never was it known, that any one who fled to thy protection, implored thy help, and sought thy intercession, was left unaided. Inspired with this confidence, I fly unto thee, O Virgin of virgins, my Mother. To thee I come: before thee I stand, sinful and sorrowful. O Mother of the Word Incarnate, despise not my petitions, but in thy mercy hear and answer. Amen.

MEMORARE TO ST. JOSEPH.

(300 days indulgence, accorded by Pope Pius IX.)

Remember, O most chaste spouse of the Virgin Mary, my amiable protector, that never was it known, that any one who invoked thy protection and implored thy help, remained without consolation. Full of confidence in thy power, I come into thy presence, and recommend myself to thee with fervour. O! thou who art called father of the Redeemer, do not disdain my prayers, but in thy mercy hear and answer me. Amen.

PRAYER "EN EGO, O BONE," ETC.

Whoever after confession and communion shall say the following prayer devoutly, and with a contrite heart, before any image of Jesus Crucified, with the intention of praying for the needs of the Church, etc. may gain the Plenary Indulgence granted for ever by Pius VII. (Decree of Ap. 10, 1821.) His Holiness Pius IX. by a decree of July 31, 1858, revoking the decree of Ap. 11, 1840, declared definitively that, to gain this Plenary Indulgence, it will henceforward be necessary to make some other prayer for the needs of the Church, as well as to go to Confession and Communion.

En ego, O bone et dulcissime Jesu, ante conspectum tuum genibus me provolvo ac maximo animi ardore te oro atque obtestor ut meum in cor vividos

O good and sweetest Jesus, before Thy face I humbly kneel, and with the greatest fervour of spirit, I pray and beseech Thee to vouchsafe to fix deep

fidei, spei, et charitatis sensus, atque veram peccatorum meorum pœnitentiam, eaque emendandi firmissimam voluntátem velis imprimere: dum magno animi affectu, et dolore tua quinque Vulnera mecum ipse considero, ac mente contemplor, illud præ oculis habens, quod jam in ore ponebat suo David Propheta de Te, O bone Jesu: "Foderunt manus meas et pedes meos; dinumeraverunt omnia ossa mea."—Ps. xxi. 17.

in my heart lively sentiments of faith, hope, and charity, true contrition for my sins, and a most firm purpose of amendment; whilst I contemplate with great sorrow and affection Thy five wounds, and ponder them over in my mind, having before my eyes the words which, long ago, David the prophet spoke in his own person concerning Thee, my Jesus: "Foderunt manus meas et pedes meos: dinumeraverunt omnia ossa mea."— "They digged My hands and My feet: they numbered all my bones."—Ps. xxi. 17, 18.

HYMN IN HONOUR OF THE AGONY OF JESUS.

The saddest night that ever fell
   Had fall'n on sinful earth,
The Son of God who made Himself
   Our Brother at His birth,

Had kept the Pasch and then had wrought
  That miracle sublime,
That makes Him on the altar dwell
  Unto the end of time.

His work on earth was done, and now
  Th' appointed hour drew nigh
When He, the Life of all that live,
  Should give Himself to die;
But ere He died the spotless Lamb
  Had still to undergo,
To save the sinners whom He loved,
  An agony of woe.

Forth from the supper-chamber then
  He took His way once more
To that same Mount of Olives, where
  He oft had gone before:
He went, for love more strong than death
  Urg'd on His willing feet;
He went, my Lord and Saviour went
  A cruel death to meet.

And with Him went the little band
  Of His disciples dear
And Jesus spake to them in words
  Of sorrow and of fear.
And Peter, James, and John, He took
  Who once on Thabor's height
Had seen His glory, and He said,
  "My heart is sad to-night."

"My heart is sorrowful to death,
  My dear disciples stay,
And in the hour of my distress
  Be with me, watch and pray:"
And then with failing steps He went
  Forward a little space,
Into a grotto near at hand
  And fell upon His face.

Alas! my Lord and Saviour dear
  What mortal heart can know
The mystery of that dread hour—
  Thine agony of woe?
The knowledge of the morrow's Cross
  Fill'd all Thy Soul with fear,
The ancient foe of God and man
  In that dark night was near.

And all the sins that men shall do,
  And all that they have done,
And all their past and future griefs
  Came forward one by one.
And Thou didst see, that, spite of all
  Thy sorrows and Thy pain,
Sinners would turn away from Thee
  And make Thy suff'rings vain.

Long time my Lord lay prostrate there
  Upon the dark, cold ground,
And as He pray'd a sweat of blood
  Moisten'd the earth around.

"My Father, let this chalice pass,"
  Thus spake God's only Son;
"But if it may not, Father, then
  Thy will, not mine, be done."

An angel forth from highest heaven
  Was sent in that sad night
To strengthen Christ the Son of God
  The angel's joy and might.
He came to those whom He had prayed
  With Him their watch to keep:
They promised they would die with Him,
  And now—they are asleep!

Alas! that Christ should turn to those
  Whom His own hands had made,
Should turn in His dread agony
  For sympathy and aid,
And find them sleeping one and all
  O'erwhelm'd with sorrow's pow'r;
He knew their weakness and He said,
  "Could ye not watch one hour?"

O dearest Lord! we pray Thee turn
  On us a pitying eye,
We are Thy children, Thou for us
  Didst agonize and die;
Alas for us! that for our sins
  Thy heart such woe should bear!
Alas for sinners who refuse
  Its tender love to share!

Thou knowest what it is to see
 The hour of death draw near,
And what it is to agonize
 In sorrow and in fear.
Thou knowest thousands at this hour
 In agony are lying,
Thou knowest when our hour will come,
 Dear Saviour, help the dying!

HYMN IN HONOUR OF THE SORROWS OF MARY.

The heart of Jesu's Mother blest
 Of Mary Queen of heaven,
While she abode upon this earth,
 Was pierc'd with sorrows seven.

How should she suffer, loved by God
 Far more than any other?
How fail to suffer—when she was
 The Man of Sorrows' Mother?

She came to bring her Child to God,
 A Mother pure and young,
Alas! the sounds of coming woe
 Fell from a prophet's tongue.

He said a sword should pierce her heart,
 O Mary from that day,
I think the cloud of grief and fear,
 Was never far away!

A few short weeks and she must fly
   Forth to a heathen land,
To save the Saviour of the world
   From Herod's impious hand.

But then came calm and peaceful years,
   Whilst Christ her life and joy,
'Neath her adoring love and care
   From infant grew to boy.

With Mary and with Joseph blest
   The paschal feast He kept,
And then they lost Him, three sad days
   They sought Him and they wept.

And even then her inmost heart
   Fore-knew those three sad days,
When He should lie within the grave
   Hid from her loving gaze.

Again the quiet peaceful years
   At Nazareth went by:
But all the while His Mother knew
   The death He had to die.

And when the awful day was come
   She met Him on the road
Bearing the Cross to Calvary,
   And falling 'neath the load.

Oh! Mary surely God on high
   Upheld thee by His might,
Else thou hadst fall'n to earth and died
   At once, at such a sight.

She did not faint, she did not fall,
  But in His steps she trod,
She saw the blood that mark'd the way
  It was the blood of God.

She saw Him stretched upon the Cross,
  She heard each cruel blow,
That nail'd His hands, and nail'd His feet
  Fast to that tree of woe.

She saw Him raised upon the Cross
  Between the earth and heav'n,
She stood there while the sun was dark,
  She heard His sayings seven.

She stood there all those three long hours,
  Close to the Cross's side,
She watch'd His suff'rings to the last,
  She liv'd while Jesus died.

She saw them take His body down
  Before the close of day,
Within her arms, as when a babe
  Once more her Jesus lay.

Alas! how terrible a change
  In her Beloved now!
The scourge has torn His sinless Flesh,
  The thorns have pierc'd His Brow.

She saw the five great open wounds
  Of Side, and Feet, and Hands,—
She help'd to wrap His lifeless Form
  In swathing funeral bands.

And then she followed those who bore
  The Fruit of her blest womb,
And buried Him with many a tear,
  In Joseph's garden tomb.

Oh! Mary, surely mother's heart
  With woes like these must break!
Oh Mary all that Jesus bore
  He bore it for our sake!

O Mary who art with thy Son
  For evermore on high,
Pray for us sinners while we live,
  Pray for us when we die!

CHAPTER XVII.
The Holy Hour.

The Holy Hour is an exercise of mental or vocal prayer, made for an hour on Thursday night at any time after nine o'clock, generally from eleven till midnight, in order to honour and to share the sorrows of Jesus in the Garden of Olives. This devotion is closely connected with devotion to the Sacred Heart of Jesus, they arose simultaneously, they have a common origin, and their object is the same; the Son of God burning with love for men and giving Himself as a sacrifice for their salvation.

The sufferings of the Heart of Jesus seem to have reached their climax in His agony in the Garden. They were so intense, that by an unheard of prodigy, He poured forth a sweat of Blood, and He said to His Apostles, *My soul is sorrowful even unto death.* He seeks compassion from those who love Him. He said to Blessed Margaret Mary Alacoque, *I request you to spend the hour from eleven to twelve o'clock of the night between Thursday and Friday in prayer, that you may share the sorrows of My Agony in the Garden, and appease My anger towards sinners.* Such was the origin of the *Holy Hour*. We know the favours by which our Lord rewarded His servant's fidelity, in practising this devotion.

We recommend the Associates of the Confraternity of the Agonizing Heart of Jesus, to keep the Holy Hour, if not every week, at least once a month. It would be well if several persons could make an arrangement together, so that it should be kept by one of them every Thursday night. This, however, is not one of the ordinary exercises of the Association, it is merely a pious practice. Those who desire to gain the indulgences attached to the Confraternity of the Holy Hour, established at Paray-le-Monial, should become members. We will say a few words of this Confraternity.

THE AGONIZING HEART OF JESUS. 125

THE CONFRATERNITY OF THE HOLY HOUR

Is established in the Monastery of the Visitation at Paray-le-Monial, in the diocese of Autun, with the view of rendering every Thursday night, a special homage of compassion to the sorrows of the Heart of Jesus during His Agony in the Garden of Olives. Those who wish to join it, should send their names to Paray-le-Monial. We give a summary of the regulations: 1st. Three persons should agree to keep the Holy Hour in turn: 2nd. They should send their names to the Monastery of the Visitation at Paray-le-Monial: 3rd. If any one of them is unable to practise this devotion on her appointed day, she should make up for the omission by uniting herself in spirit to the sufferings of our Lord in His Agony. When one of the three is removed by death or any other cause, the vacant place should be filled up. 4th. The Holy Hour may be kept at any time after sunset, in Church or elsewhere. 5th. A member of a religious community, is not required to join with two other persons, but need merely send her name to Paray-le-Monial, and keep the Holy Hour at the time selected by her Superior. Farther information regarding the Confraternity and the indulgences attached to it, can be had from the Superior of the Visitation at Paray-le-Monial, near Autun,

(Saône.) There is also a little book called the Holy Hour, by Father Debrosse.

PRAYER TO JESUS IN HIS AGONY.
Which may be used during the Holy Hour.

O my Saviour Jesus, who, for the great love which Thou bearest to all men, didst will to be "*sorrowful even unto death,*" in the Garden of Olives; and in Thy heaviness and Agony didst deign to be comforted by an Angel, do not reject the consolation which I, Thy most unworthy servant, offer to Thee, with all possible love and veneration. Alas! my sweetest Saviour, I was one of the causes of Thine Agony; for me Thou didst suffer; for me Thou didst pour forth a sweat of Blood, Thy tears and sighs were on my account. O my Jesus, let me unite my prayer to Thy prayer, my sacrifice to Thy sacrifice, for the expiation of my sins, and the salvation of the souls of the dying; and then let me join the Angel in consoling Thee in Thine Agony. Let me be with Thee in the lonely grotto, let me witness Thine Agonies, let me compassionate and share them, and drink with Thee even to the dregs, the chalice of bitterness which Thy Father has given Thee. Glorious Minister of the most High, whose sublime mission it was to console and strengthen God, let me with thee, keep my Saviour company. Would that I could also give some consolation to His heaviness and mortal agony! Give me thy strength, thy courage, thy love, that I may *pray* with Jesus, *suffer* with Jesus, and *die* with and for Jesus. Amen.

PRAYERS OF BLESSED MARGARET MARY ALACOQUE TO THE SACRED HEART OF JESUS.

I.—*Act of Adoration to the Sacred Heart of Jesus.*

I adore Thy Sovereignty, O sacred and divine Heart of Jesus, with all the powers of my soul. I desire to love Thee, to fear Thee and to honour Thee, I will take the greatest care never to offend Thee, because I love Thee and wish to love Thee more than all things, and with all my strength. I detest all mortal sin and all deliberate venial sin; I hope that as I am entirely Thine, as Thou didst give me life upon the Cross amid Thy sufferings, Thou wilt take pity on my weakness and misery and never let me perish.

Most loving Heart! I offer myself to Thee, with the intention of loving, of honouring and glorifying Thee by my whole being, by my life, by every one of my sufferings and actions. I love Thee as my Sovereign Good, my sole joy, the only object of the worship and love of all hearts. Let my heart be consumed by the fire of pure love. I now renew with my whole soul all the offerings which I have ever made of myself to Thee. Keep me from ever displeasing Thee, and make me ever to do that which is most agreeable to Thee.

Fountain of love! I would that I were all heart to love Thee, and all mind to adore Thee! Let me love nothing except in Thee and for Thy sake. Let my memory dwell only upon Thee; let my understanding be entirely occupied with Thee; let my will and affections have Thee for their only object; let my feet do nothing but seek Thee; my tongue speak only to praise Thee; my eyes look only at Thee, and my hands do nothing but serve Thee, so that I may love Thee throughout eternity. Amen.

II.—*Consecration to the Sacred Heart of Jesus.*

I, N. N. give and consecrate to the Sacred Heart of our Lord Jesus Christ, myself, my life, my actions, my trials and sufferings, so that I will henceforth do nothing but love, honour, and glorify It. My constant purpose is to be entirely devoted to It, to do everything for Its love, and to give up everything that displeases It.

O Sacred Heart! I choose Thee for the only object of my love, the protector of my life, the assurance of my salvation, the remedy of my weakness, the repairer of all my failings; be my sure refuge at the hour of death. Most merciful Heart be my justification before God, and turn away His anger from me. Most loving Heart, I place all my confidence in Thee, I fear everything from my own wickedness, but I hope everything from Thy goodness. Consume in me everything that can displease Thee or resist Thee; let Thy pure love take such possession of my heart, that I may never forget Thee nor be separated from Thee. I pray Thee by Thine infinite goodness, that my name may be written on Thee, since I would live and die Thy servant. Amen.

III.—*Act of charity in contemplation of our Saviour's wounded side.*

My Saviour, place me in Thy Heart, which is a furnace of love, and then I shall be safe. O Jesus, my Sovereign Good, I hope for entrance there, for I love Thee not for the sake of reward, but for love of Thee. I love Thee above all that is lovely, above all goodness, above all beauty, more than all men, more than all pleasures, more than myself, more than all that is not Thee, and I protest before heaven and earth, that I wish to live and die in Thy love. And if for my love of Thee I were to be persecuted and tormented, and even to suffer death, I would be very glad, and I will always say with St. Paul: no creature is able to separate me from the Sacred Heart of my Jesus, whom I love and will love for ever. O most loving Heart, Thou art my strength and support! O most adorable Heart! Thou art my refuge, my salvation, my reward, my love, and my all. Amen.

IV.—*Blessed Margaret Mary Alacoque's compact with the Sacred Heart of Jesus.*

(May be used by any one, it contains acts of pure love.)

With a contrite and humble heart I offer Thee my homage of love, praise, and adoration, O most divine Heart of Jesus, acknowledging Thy sovereign rights over my soul, and confirming every promise of fidelity to Thee that I have ever made......I wish to do this as many times as I draw my breath, for I am, and will be Thine, spite of all the opposition of the enemies of my salvation. I renounce and disavow every suggestion contrary to the pure love of Thee. O Sacred Heart, reject me not, but acknowledge me as Thine own. Receive me and defend me, strengthen my weakness, for my great desire is to love and serve Thee; give me grace to do it perfectly. Therefore, O most loving Heart, I give Thee my body, my soul, my heart, and all that I am, to love and glorify Thee. I wish to repeat this donation by all my words, and I wish that every movement of my lips might be an act of contrition for all the sins I have done, and all the good that I have neglected to do. O most loving Heart, would that I could draw Thee unto myself every time I draw in my breath, and that every time I give it forth I could offer Thee to Thine Eternal Father, to pay Him all I owe. I would offer Thee every beating of my heart as an act of love and gratitude for all the gifts and graces that I have received or shall receive from Thee. Take away, I pray Thee, every thing that hinders me from corresponding to them.

I would fain go nearer to Thee by every step I take, I wish that my every movement might show Thee my desire to be united to Thee, so as never again to be separated from Thee. Grant that everything I understand may lead me to love Thee, and that every glance of my eyes may invite Thee to come into my heart and take possession of me, so as to transform me into Thyself.

For the same end I offer Thee every morsel I eat, to be like a Spiritual Communion; and let what I drink be like the living water of Thy grace, which purifies me from all my sins, and from every thing in me that displeases Thee.

O Most Sacred, Divine and Adorable Heart! receive and accept this compact which I make with Thee, and which I mean to render as often as I put my hand on my heart, or kiss the cross; renouncing every suggestion of pride and self-love, and every inordinate movement of nature, protesting a thousand times that I am entirely Thine, and that if I knew of any more perfect way of uniting myself to Thee, I would follow it, even at the cost of my life. O Divine Heart of Jesus, do not let my sleep or anything else interrupt this agreement which I would have endure until my last breath.

I wish to live and die in the arms of my Crucified Saviour, and to hide myself in His Divine Heart. Amen.

V.—*To the Heart of Jesus.*

O Divine Heart, loving Heart, Heart devoted to the love of man! I wish to have a heart only to make a return of love to Thee, and to give myself entirely to Thee for ever. O Wound flowing with water and Blood for my healing, my heart is wounded by the sight of so many sorrows and mysteries. O Jesus, receive my heart into the open Wound which has been made by the lance, and by Thy love in Thy Sacred Side! There is room enough for it there, there is room for all human hearts. Thou dost not despise a broken heart, I pray Thee that my heart may be broken with grief, so that it may enter into Thine, and become one with it, and if it is not pure enough, take it away that I may live no more to myself, and give me a new one that I may live by a new life; give me Thy Heart, that I may live for Thee alone. O I will love nothing in comparison with the Heart which has loved me more than Its life. I say it in presence of the Divine Majesty which beholds me from the Throne of glory in Heaven; of the Blessed Virgin whose Heart was full of love for her Divine Son, and of all the Saints who find their bliss in the Heart of Jesus. I consecrate to its honour, my understanding, my memory, my will, my body, my soul, and all that I am, and I renounce everything that might hinder this consecration. O Heart of Jesus, Adorable Heart, greatest and holiest of all hearts, I leave all for Thee, and as Thou art all mine, I will be all Thine throughout eternity. Amen.

ASPIRATIONS OF LOVE.

By St. Mary Magdalen of Pazzi.

Burning with divine love, she would exclaim; "O love! love! O God of love! Thy love for Thy creatures is too great. Yet no, my Jesus! it is not too much for Thy greatness, but too much for their nothingness and vileness. O my Saviour! why dost Thou give me so much love?"

Sometimes with a crucifix in her hand, she would run through the monastery, speaking words of such ardent love, that all the sisters were inflamed by them. "O love!" she would say, "O love! love! my God I will never cease to call Thee my love, my hope, and my all." Then turning to the others she would ask them, "did you not know, dear sisters, that my Jesus is nothing but love?"—At other times the Spirit of God impelled her with irresistible force, and she used to go through the garden and the cloister, and when she met one of the sisters would say to her: "Soul! do you love God as much as your own life? Are you not burning and dying with love?"

Her love was not only ardent, but effective, that is to say, it was shown by her works. To please God she took the greatest pains to preserve perfect purity of soul and body, and she directed all her actions to His greater glory. She said, "If I knew that by saying a single word for any other object than God's glory, without offending Him, I could become greater than a Seraph, I would not say it." Her delight was in doing the holy will of God; and her horror of sin was so great, that a few days before her death she said, "I leave this world without having been able to understand how a creature can ever consent to sin against its Creator." Pious reader, have a great devotion to St. Mary Magdalen of Pazzi, you will not fail to experience the good effects of her powerful protection.

CHAPTER XVIII.

Easy Method of Meditation.

1. The evening before, prepare the subject attentively, making use of some good book of Meditation, or the Gospel, or the *Following of Christ.*

2. When you are going to bed, recall briefly to mind the subject and heads of the Meditation.

3. Do this again on waking in the morning, as soon as you have offered your heart and your day to God and to the Agonizing Heart of Jesus.

4. Make your meditation in Church, or some quiet place.

5. Kneel down, and before beginning your meditation, make the *preparatory prayer*, and the *prelude.* For the *preparatory prayer*, adore God present; ask pardon of your sins by an act of contrition; offer Him your meditation, the works and sufferings of the day for His greater glory and for the salvation of souls, especially of those who are to die this day. For the *prelude*, imagine that you see Jesus, or His Blessed Mother, or the angels, or saints before you, with their eyes fixed upon you—or make a picture of

any circumstance bearing on the subject of your meditation. Then place definitely before your mind, and pray God to give you the grace you want, viz: light to understand that on which you are about to meditate, and strength to practise the resolutions you will make. This prayer will vary with the subject of the meditation. For instance, if you are meditating on mortal sin, ask *light* to know its malice, its evil consequences, the punishment deserved by it... and *strength* to defeat it and avoid it in future. If you are meditating on Jesus in Agony in the Garden, ask *light* to understand the sorrows He endured, and the virtues He practised, especially His patience, humility, and entire conformity to the Holy Will of God:—and *strength* to have compassion with those sorrows, and to imitate those virtues especially such as you most need.

6. Then enter on what is called the body of the meditation; take the different points in order, and *first, use your memory* to recall the first point to your mind, or if you have forgotten it, refer to the book. 2nd. *Apply your understanding* to this point. Reflect simply and deeply on the truth or truths before you; and ask the Holy Spirit to suggest wholesome thoughts. 3rd. *Apply your will and heart* to the truth before you, feed your soul with it by acts of holy affection, strengthen the good resolutions you have made by exercising a disposition to do any-

thing that God requires of you, and by sorrow for all your past failings. If the Holy Spirit speaks to your heart, listen to His voice and obey it. When you have finished one point, proceed to the others in the same way.

7 Conclude by a colloquy with our Lord, or His Blessed Mother, or the angels, or saints... as your devotion may lead you. This colloquy ought to be full of humility, piety, affection, and confidence.

8. Make some practical resolution, bearing reference to your chief fault, to the performance of your duties, or the acquirement of some virtue, especially of humility. End by a *Pater Noster... Ave Maria*, and the prayer, *O most merciful Jesus.*

Note.—We give two meditations on the *Agony of Jesus in the Garden of Olives*, and on *His continual sorrows throughout His mortal life*, which may also serve for spiritual reading. They are divided into paragraphs, each one of which may form a point of meditation, and might be used with advantage on the last Friday of each month, on the day of *monthly intercession*, and during the triduum in preparation for the *annual intercession.*

FIRST MEDITATION.

On the Agony of the Heart of Jesus in the Garden of Olives.

I. In order to estimate the sorrows of Jesus in His Agony, we must first know the greatness of His love. His love for His Father is infinite, and He sees Him infinitely offended by men. His love for men is excessive, and He sees that their guilt is excessive, and that eternal punishment awaits them. What pain for the most tender of all hearts! He longs, at any cost, to repair the outrage against His Father; and to deliver men from the chastisement they deserve, by suffering in their stead. O My Father, He says, all men together are unable to satisfy Thy justice; all the victims they could offer are unworthy of Thee. Here I am, let the blow fall on Me.

II. The Eternal Father accepts the offering made by His Son; He lays all the iniquities of men upon Him, and from that moment looks on Him as one under a curse, covered with all the crimes of the world. At the same time Jesus Christ felt the full weight of that fearful burden. What a bitter chalice the Saint of Saints has to drink! Will He indeed drink it? As soon as it touches His sacred Lips, His Soul is overwhelmed by unspeakable grief; He falls into the deepest sadness; He is oppressed with heaviness and weariness; He is full of fear. He prays, *Father, remove this chalice from me: nevertheless not My will, but Thine be done.* Alas! my Jesus must drink it to the very dregs.

III. He submits to the good pleasure of God, His Father; His grief increases, and He would fain share it with His apostles. He had already said to them, *My soul is sorrowful even unto death.* But they have succumbed to their own sorrow, and during their Master's mortal agony they are asleep. Jesus comes, pale and trembling, to seek some consolation from them, and to strengthen them against their fears. Alas! He finds them asleep. What! could you not watch one hour with me? Watch and pray, lest you enter into temptation. Jesus returns to the grotto of the agony, He prays again, His desolation is greater than ever. He goes back to His apostles; they are asleep. He prays again to His Father, but His Father answers not.

IV. Then Jesus gives Himself up to all the bitterness of grief. The love which fills His Divine Heart unites with His Father's severity to punish the sin with which He is loaded. He wishes to suffer mental tortures a thousand times more intense than the bodily tortures about to be inflicted on Him by the cruelty of His murderers. He, therefore, allows His imagination to represent to Him in the most forcible manner the causes of His Passion and Death. He sees all the powers of hell let loose against Him, He sees the bolts of Divine Justice ready to fall on His head, He sees all sinners in arms against Him, He beholds all the sins and iniquities of all ages and places concentrated on Him. Judas' treachery, Peter's denial, the flight of all His disciples, the reproaches, the blasphemies, the mockeries, the bonds, the scourges, the thorns, the cross, the nails, are all before Him. And, worst of all, He sees that His death will be of no avail to multitudes; that His Blood will be trampled under foot, His holy mysteries profaned, His Church persecuted, rent by schisms and heresies, saddened and dishonoured by the scandals of her children. He sees the countless human beings who pass each day into eternity, many of them, alas! in a state of mortal sin. Yet more, He saw me amongst His murderers, each one of my sins passed before Him, as a cause of His death, and added its share to His sorrows.

V. He loses Himself, He goes down yet deeper into this ocean of desolation. He is motionless, He sighs deeply, He weeps, He stops weeping, grief seems to have dried up the very source of tears. His voice is weak and failing, He speaks in broken words, Father, Father, have pity on Thy Son, remove this chalice from me.

VI. But again, the mighty love of His compassionate Heart overcomes all the repugnance of nature. His Father has been offended...men, His brethren are perishing! Is not this enough to make Him drink the chalice of bitterness to the very dregs? Yes, My Father, avenge Thyself. Punish in me, the sin of Thine ungrateful and rebellious creature, man. Let Thy Son satisfy Thy justice. Do not regard the shrinking of my nature. O Father, Thy Will, not mine be done!

VII. Alas! His sufferings become more and more fearful. O Christians, admire the gentleness, the obedience, the submission, the ardent charity of this innocent Victim. Have compassion on His sorrows and anguish. Behold the tender Lamb of God! His eyes are sunk, His face is deadly pale, His soul seems to hover on His lips, He is in agony. And what an agony, O my God! His Blood is driven back to His Heart and almost stops its pulsations, but His strong and generous love keeps Him alive, that He may suffer yet more, and consummate His Sacrifice upon the Cross. It drives the Blood back from His Heart to seek an outlet in every pore of His body. His glorious Face, His Hands and Feet are covered with it; the earth around is moistened by it. O sweat of Blood, I adore Thee! cleanse me from all my sins, cleanse all the sinners upon earth who are now in their agony and are to die to-day. O Jesus, let all the dying to the end of time feel the quickening power of the Blood which Thou hast shed forth drop by drop for the salvation of the human race. O most Holy Virgin, apply the merits of that Divine Blood to our souls; teach us to persevere in prayer, to suffer with patience and submission that we may be like Thy dear Son Jesus in the Garden of Olives.

SECOND MEDITATION.

On the continual sorrows of the Heart of Jesus during the whole course of His mortal life.

(From the Bollandist Lives of the Saints, Blessed Angela of Foligno, Chap. xiv.)

I. Blessed Angela of Foligno, had a special light from the Holy Spirit to enable her to understand these sorrows—we give her own words: "The whole life of Jesus Christ was a most bitter penance...From the time that His Soul was created and united to His most holy Body in the womb of the Immaculate Virgin, until it was separated from the same most holy Body in His cruel death on the Cross, Jesus Christ was never without that compassion;" that is without most bitter penance.

II. Consider the companions which God the Father willed His Beloved Son to have in this world: first, the most entire, continual and extreme poverty; secondly, the most entire, continual and extreme contempt; and thirdly, the most entire, continual and extreme sorrow. "Such were the society in which He spent His whole life."

The Saint gives a further explanation of the extreme poverty and humiliations which accompanied our Lord throughout His whole life, and then proceeds to speak of His extreme sorrow.

III. The third companion of Jesus Christ was the extreme sorrow which was with His Soul from the moment of its union with His most holy Body. At that very moment it was filled with the greatest sadness...In the womb of His Virgin Mother, Jesus began to suffer, for He saw and understood all that He was to undergo in Soul and in Body for our sakes. The foresight of His approaching death caused Him such agony that His Body poured forth a sweat of Blood, and His Soul has already suffered the greatest grief before His Body shared it.

IV. " Jesus Christ could not be without sorrow, when He thought that He was to be sold, betrayed, seized, denied, forsaken, bound, buffeted, mocked, smitten, accused, blasphemed, cursed, scourged, judged, condemned, led like a malefactor to crucifixion, stripped, nailed to the Cross, and pierced with a lance."...All these things were ever present to His holy Soul, and must have caused Him the greatest sadness, and this sadness was life-long. "Our Lord Jesus Christ endured countless sorrows. At His birth He was laid on straw, in a stable, in a hard manger, between two animals, and so from the very first He began to bear bodily afflictions..."

V. As a man, immediately after His Baptism He went to the desert, He there fasted forty days, and was hungry...Afterwards He journeyed on foot through the towns and villages, bearing hunger, thirst, wet, heat, and cold, He was often wearied and covered with sweat, He endured all kinds of discomfort, and at last death-itself.

VI. As to the sorrows of His Passion, no heart can conceive them, no tongue can describe them. The grief of Christ was complex; His compassion for the human race which He loved so dearly, caused Him intense suffering. It was not a mere general compassion for the whole race, but an individual compassion for each man. If we could know the number of the whole race, and the number of the sins of each one, we might then know the number of sorrows which the mercy and compassion of Christ led Him to endure. It is manifest that His sorrow was extreme and infinite, for He loved each one of His elect in an ineffable manner, and because of that love He felt their offences and the pains they were to endure for them...The sorrow and compassion of our most loving Jesus made Him bear the torments of the Cross, and undergo a dreadful death in order that He might satisfy for our offences and might redeem us...

VII. His compassion for Himself was another cause of His sorrow. He saw that His Father had sent Him to bear in His own Person the griefs and pains of all His elect, that He had been given entirely to us for this end, and therefore He had compassion on Himself, and this compassion was full of sorrow. If anyone knew that a great affliction was certainly coming upon him, and had the thought of it constantly before him, undoubtedly he would have compassion on himself, and his sufferings in anticipation would be in proportion to the greatness of the coming trouble. ...Now this was the case with Jesus Christ, more fully than I can express.

VIII. "The compassion of Jesus Christ for His most merciful Father, was another cause of His sorrow. He loved His Father with an infinite love, He saw Him so full of compassion and mercy for us as to be willing to deliver up His well-beloved Son to death for our sakes, and therefore, He in His turn was filled with compassion and infinite grief. And this grief is one that we cannot express. Therefore I say, grief dwelt with Jesus Christ in an ineffable manner, by the permission and dispensation of the ineffable Wisdom of God. And the more intense the sorrow, the more wonderful is the divine dispensation; so that the sorrow is beyond the comprehension of any created intelligence. This divine dispensation was the origin of all the sorrows of Christ; and as our understanding cannot comprehend the infinite charity of Jesus Christ in redeeming us by His death, neither can it comprehend the infinite sorrow which He suffered in virtue of the divine dispensation." The supernatural light given to Christ was another cause of sorrow...It showed Him the vast measure of grief assigned to Him, of grief so surpassing that it was hidden from every creature.

IX. Again, Jesus Christ sorrowed from compassion for His most holy Mother, whom He loved more than any creature, because He had received from her His virginal Flesh, and because she, above all others, shared His sufferings. He saw His holy Mother endure the greatest sufferings of body and soul, and His compassion for her made Him suffer the same. The grief of His Mother was extreme, and Christ bore it in His own Heart, in obedience to the Divine dispensation.

X. "Jesus Christ sorrowed because His Father whom He loved above all things, was offended. He saw that when men crucified Him, their Lord and Creator, an infinite offence was offered to God the Father. The Crucifixion of the Son of God was the greatest of all possible sins, and therefore God was more offended by it than by any other; and this was a cause of immense sorrow to Christ. And it may be, that God the Father would have condemned the whole human race afresh for this enormous crime, but for the touching prayer of our Lord, who forgot His own griefs to plead for His murderers."

XI. Jesus Christ sorrowed because of His compassion for His apostles and disciples. They and the women who followed Him were overwhelmed with grief, and as He loved them most tenderly He bore it in His own Heart.

XII. Our Lord had many other sorrows, and the nobility of His Soul made them the more intense; they were acute in proportion to the holiness and tenderness of His Soul. His mental sufferings in their turn affected His Body, and as that virginal Body was more noble than any other born of woman, it was also more sensible to suffering. Again, He was God, the Second Person of the Blessed Trinity, and therefore every injury done to Him was an infinite offence, and an infinite cause of suffering.

XIII. And amidst all these sufferings, the Saviour of the world, the God-man Christ Jesus, uttered no word of threatening or malediction, He did not defend Himself nor avenge Himself; when He was accused, He did not justify Himself; when they spit upon His Face, He did not cover it; when they stretched out His Hands and Arms, He did not withdraw them; when they sought Him to put Him to death, He did not hide Himself, but gave Himself up to their will, that He might accomplish the work of our redemption. What tenderness! what surpassing mercy! what incomprehensible goodness! Where infinite iniquity abounds, infinite grace abounds.

XIV. After having dwelt on our Saviour's sufferings, the Saint exhorts us all to follow His footsteps, and to bear our Cross after His. She shows the great value of tribulation borne for the love of Jesus Christ, and thus concludes, "A soul that looks at the beloved Jesus, and has even a little love for Him ought to desire nothing in the world but what He had;—sorrow, anguish, and affliction." Dear reader, this doctrine is very high and difficult to practise; but never forget that God's grace is all-powerful, and that nothing is impossible to the love of God joined with humility and confidence.

METHOD OF HEARING MASS,

In union with the Agonizing Heart of Jesus.

No exercise of our holy religion gives such glory to God as the Sacrifice of the Mass, which is at the same time of the greatest value for our salvation and that of the dying. In this sacrifice of love the Heart of Jesus offers itself anew to His Father; and we ought to pay it a special honour, by assisting at that sacrifice, by union with its intentions and dispositions, by conformity to its desires, by recollection of its virtues, sufferings, and charity, and by an ardent return of love.

Offering of the Holy Mass.

Almighty and Eternal God, in the Holy Sacrifice of the Mass a worthy homage is offered to Thine infinite greatness. Thy Divine Son, at once Priest and Victim, is about to sacrifice Himself upon this Altar. I firmly believe this truth, and in order to please Thy Divine Majesty I unite myself to this Holy Victim. O Lord, receive the offering of my whole being along with that of the Heart of Thy beloved Son.
☦ O Agonizing Heart of my Jesus, I offer Thee this august sacrifice, to honour Thine infinite sufferings and perfections, to thank Thee for the many graces Thou hast bestowed upon me, to implore forgiveness for all my faults, and to obtain from Thy bounty, especially the grace of ...... O most merciful Heart, deign to apply to me and to all the agonizing the merits and the fruit of this Divine Sacrifice, and accept the offering which I make to Thee of my own heart.

At the beginning of Mass.

Surely our hearts would have been full of love and respect if we had seen Jesus Christ offering Himself on Calvary's height, and shedding His Blood for us on the Cross! In a few moments this great sacrifice will be renewed on this altar, and every day it is renewed at once in thousands of places.

Yes, my dear Saviour, spite of all the fury of hell, Thy prophet's words are fulfilled; "from the rising of the sun even to the going down, Thy name is great among the Gentiles, and in every place there is sacrifice, and there is offered to Thy name a clean oblation." And of Thine infinite goodness, this oblation, which is Thyself, is offered for me and for all the faithful, upon our altars.

O innocent Victim, I see Thee laden with my iniquities, and those of the whole world. Thou hast shed bitter tears for them, Thou hast expiated them by most grievous sufferings, and by a most cruel death. O tender Lamb, let me mingle my tears with Thine. I confess to Thee, to Blessed Mary ever Virgin, and to all Thy saints, that I have sinned, and that my sins have wounded Thine Heart, have shed Thy Blood, and caused Thy death. O most merciful Jesus, by Thy tears, by Thy sufferings, by Thine agony, by Thy death, by the Blood and the wound of Thy Divine Heart, mercifully grant us pardon, absolution and remission of all our sins.

At the Introit.

O Lord Thou hast pity on all poor sinners who turn to Thee with confidence, hear our cries, listen to our supplications, have compassion on our sorrows. Receive the worship which we offer Thee with a contrite and humble heart. We wish that we could dispose of the hearts of all men, that we might offer them to Thee. May our adorations and our love be as agreeable to Thee as if we offered Thee thousands of victims!

At the Kyrie Eleison.

Divine Creator of our souls, have mercy on the work of Thine own Hands. Most merciful Father, have mercy on Thy children, especially on those who are this day to appear before Thine awful tribunal.

O Jesus, Son of God, author of our salvation, who, not contented with offering Thyself once for us on Calvary, dost ever continue to offer Thyself on our altar, have mercy on us, have mercy on the dying: let us all have a share in the merit of Thine agony, of Thy death, and of Thy Precious Blood.

Holy Spirit, Sanctifier and Comforter, have mercy on us, have mercy on the dying; descend again on earth, and inflame all hearts with Thy holy love. Protect the holy Church, our Mother, and the Sovereign Pontiff, our Father. Send us saints, men powerful in word and in work. Put an end to our tribulations.

At the Gloria in Excelsis.

O God! I am not fit to praise Thee! but united to the Agonizing Heart of Thy Son Jesus, I offer Thee adoration, thanksgiving, and praise worthy of Thee. Honour, glory, and dominion be to Thee, O Lord, and to that Adorable Heart, throughout all ages. Amen.

At the Dominus Vobiscum.

O God of all goodness, fill Thy ministers with Thy Spirit, that they may be worthy of Thine Heart. Give them a holy zeal for Thy glory and for our salvation, and great fortitude to endure the weariness attendant on their labours.

At the Collects.

O God of infinite mercy! we pray Thee to look upon the Heart of Thy Beloved Son Jesus, that appeased by the sight of the sorrows it endured, especially in the Garden of Olives and on the Cross, Thou mayest grant us the pardon of our sins, and put an end to the ills which afflict us.

By that Sacred Heart have pity on the many souls that are perishing, above all, have pity on the dying; succour Thy Church and remove her tribulations. Restore to us Thine ancient mercies. Do not reject our beloved country, which Jesus Christ redeemed by His own Blood.

O Mary, help of Christians, we pray thee by thy compassionate Heart to come to our assistance and to reconcile us to thy Divine Son.

Glorious Saint Joseph, nursing Father of Jesus, chaste husband of Mary, intercede for us. Thou art the Patron of a good death, pray for those who are in their agony. Saint Michael, archangel, holy guardian angels, all ye Saints of Heaven, especially our glorious patrons, beseech our Lord to have mercy upon us, to open the treasures of His Heart to us, to preserve our faith, and hope, and charity, and to bring us after death to a happy eternity.

At the Epistle.

Speak, Lord, Thy servant heareth; condescend to speak to me as to Thy prophets and apostles. My soul, listen to the words of the Lord.

Cease to do perversely, learn to do well. Neither the adulterers, nor thieves, nor drunkards,

nor railers, shall possess the kingdom of God.
Fly these things, and pursue justice, godliness,
faith, charity, patience, mildness. Labour for
heaven, and that you may gain it, walk worthy
of God, in all things pleasing; being fruitful in
every good work, and increasing in the knowledge
of God; loving one another with the charity of
brotherhood. In carefulness not slothful. In
spirit fervent. Serving the Lord. Patient in
tribulations. Instant in prayer. Honour those
that are above you. Fear God. Cleave to the
shepherd and bishop of your souls.

At the Gradual.

O God! write these truths on my heart, and
give me grace to practise them. Heal the
corruption of my heart, and let me draw near to
Thee by following Thy virtues.

O good Shepherd, have pity on Thy sheep,
seek the lost, bring back the wanderers, heal the
sick, strengthen the weak, preserve those whom
Thou hast led into Thy fold. I pray specially
for all those who are to die to-day.

O Lord forgive Thy people and do not let
Thine inheritance fall into contempt. Save us,
and we will never cease to sing Thy praises.

At the Gospel.

O Lord Thou hast the words of eternal life, let my heart receive them. Tell me what Thou wouldst have me to do.

If ye love me, says our Lord, keep my commandments. If any man will come after me, let him deny himself, and take up his cross, and follow me. Thou shalt love the Lord thy God, with thy whole heart, and with thy whole soul, and with thy whole mind, and with thy whole strength. Thou shalt love thy neighbour as thyself. Love your enemies: do good to them that hate you; and pray for them that persecute you. As you would that men should do to you, do you also to them in like manner. Judge not that you may not be judged. Take heed that no man seduce you. Watch and pray. Blessed are they that suffer persecution for justice sake. Fear ye not them that kill the body, and are not able to kill the soul; but rather fear Him that can destroy both soul and body into hell. Every one that shall confess me before men, I will also confess him before my Father who is in heaven. Beware of false prophets. He that entereth in by the door is the shepherd of the sheep; he that entereth not by the door, the same is a thief and a robber. He that shall persevere unto the end, he shall be saved.

At the Credo.

I believe, O my God, all the truths which Thou hast revealed to Thy Church. I protest that I will live and die in this faith. Grant, O Lord, that my life may be consistent with my faith, and that my faith may always be animated by good works. Let me never be ashamed to declare myself a Catholic, give me strength and courage, that I may always, and by word and by deed, uphold the interests of our holy religion.

O holy Church of Rome, the persecutions which thou dost endure, far from weakening my faith, do but strengthen it the more, since Thy Divine Spouse foretold them. How unhappy are they who separate themselves from thee! I vow inviolable attachment to thee. Lord, draw closer the bonds that bind me to Thy holy Church, in its bosom I will live and die. Amen.

At the Offertory.

Sin had ruined us, O God, and made us Thine enemies; but Jesus Christ, Thy Son, has saved us and reconciled us to Thee. It is in the Sacred Heart that this reconciliation is accomplished; His death on the Cross and the shedding of His Blood has put away our iniquities, and now, by an excess of love He renews this divine Sacrifice for us every day. His Blood is not indeed shed with violence and suffering as on Calvary, but it is really in the Chalice, it flows into our hearts, it is united to our blood, and it becomes the pledge of eternal life to us.

O my soul, admire the infinite kindness of the Heart of Jesus; consider the price at which He has redeemed thee. It is not silver or gold, but His own Blood. O marvel of mercy and love! God sacrifices Himself for me! Is it not just that I should sacrifice myself for Him? Yes, my Saviour, I will sacrifice myself with, and for Thee. But first purify and sanctify me, that I may be worthy to present myself to Thee, and to offer Thee a sweet smelling sacrifice.

O Agonizing Heart of Jesus! undying furnace of love, inflame me, consume me with Thy holy fire. I offer myself to Thee as a victim of love, entirely consecrated to Thy service.

O Agonizing Heart of Jesus! from the first moment of my existence until this day, Thou hast constantly loaded me with benefits. I offer myself to Thee as a sacrifice of thanksgiving. How much I owe Thee, my dearest Saviour, Thou hast regenerated me in Thy Holy Church, out of which there is no salvation; Thou hast strengthened me by Thy Divine Sacrament, Thou hast fed me with Thy Flesh, refreshed me with Thy Blood, and admitted me among the worshippers and friends of Thy Heart; and even now, spite of all my ingratitude, Thou watchest over me, and preparest for me an eternity of bliss. O! let me ever give thanks to Thee for Thy mercies and Thy love.

O Agonizing Heart of Jesus! my unfaithfulness was the cause of Thy sorrow throughout Thy mortal life, and of Thy cruel agony on the Mount of Olives and on the Cross. I offer myself to Thee as a victim of expiation. Make me follow Thee, O adorable Victim, that I may suffer with Thee, and like Thy holy apostle Paul, may fill up in my flesh that which is wanting of Thy sufferings.

O Agonizing Heart of my Jesus! Thy Sacrifice was not for me alone, but for all men. Ought not I also, after Thine example, to offer myself as a victim for the salvation of my brethren? O my Redeemer, I am ready, with the help of Thy grace, to suffer and to die in order to obtain for them all, and especially for those who are united to me by the ties of blood, the grace of a holy life, and a holy death.

At the Preface.

O my soul, listen to the solemn invitation of the priest. Lift up your hearts, *Sursum corda:* Let us give thanks to the Lord our God. *Gratias agamus Domino Deo nostro.* We have been created to the image of God, we have been redeemed by the Blood of His Son, why should our hearts cleave to earth? Is not the Christian's heart greater than this earth? Is it not made for God alone? Let us raise ourselves up to God, who is infinite in goodness, justice, and power, who brought us out of nothing, and could by one breath annihilate us. How great is our God! Let us fall down before Him and adore Him. The seraphim and cherubim, the angels and archangels, and all the hosts of heaven, prostrate themselves before His Throne and adore Him, and praise Him for ever. Let us join our voices to theirs, and say, Holy, Holy, Holy, Lord God of Sabaoth. Heaven and earth are full of Thy glory. Blessed is he that cometh in the name of the Lord. Glory be to God on High.

At the Canon.

Let us collect all the powers of our soul. In a few moments the sacrifice will be consummated. The Son of God made man will descend on the altar, and there, really present in the hands of the priest by virtue of the words of consecration, He will offer Himself anew for us poor sinners. O mystery of faith! marvel of mercy and of love! who can fail to love a God who is so kind and loving! (Here close your book, and give your heart up to sentiments of wonder, of humility, and of love, at the thought of this great and awful mystery. At the memento of the living, pray for the Sovereign Pontiff, for the Church, for your neighbours, for the dying, etc.)

At the Elevation.

At the Elevation of the Host and the Chalice, bow yourself down humbly, adore Him whom the angels adore, before whom they veil their faces, for He is present on the altar. He is the only Son of God, made man for us by the operation of the Holy Spirit in the chaste womb of the Blessed Virgin Mary; He is true God and true man, He was born at Bethlehem, He died on Calvary. He rose again the third day, He is now in heaven, on the throne of His glory, and on this Altar, the throne of His love. O my God, my King, my Saviour Jesus, I adore Thee, I love Thee, I pray Thee to bless me.

After the Consecration.

Jesus is here under the Sacramental species, they really contain His Body and Blood, His Soul and Divinity. I believe it, O holy Redeemer, and I am ready to give my blood to confess this faith. Would that the hearts and lives of all men were mine, that I might offer them to Thee! Thou art the King of all hearts, Thou art the Sovereign Ruler of the world. Be pleased to accept the sacrifice of my heart and life. I offer it in acknowledgment of Thy rights over every creature, as a token of my love to Thee, and in the hope of obtaining mercy for myself, for those dear to me, and for all the dying.

At the Memento of the Dead.

O Lord Jesus let the virtue of this divine sacrifice reach all members of Thy mystical Body, the Church, not only those who are still waging their warfare in this world, but also all those who have gone before us with the sign of faith, and who are in the place of expiation, awaiting their complete deliverance. Dear Jesus, mercifully hasten the moment they long for. Put an end to their sufferings, and grant them eternal rest. I pray particularly for the most forsaken souls in purgatory, for those who on earth were most devoted to Thine Agonizing Heart, and for N. N.

At the Pater.

Our Father, who art in heaven, hallowed be Thy name, Thy kingdom come, Thy will be done on earth, as it is in heaven, give us this day our daily bread, and forgive us our trespasses, as we forgive them that trespass against us, and lead us not into temptation, but deliver us from evil.

At the end of the Pater.

Deliver us, O Lord, from all evils, past, present, and to come. Let Thy right hand put to flight the enemies of Thy Holy Name, and of our salvation. O Immaculate Virgin, all ye holy apostles, angels and saints, intercede for us, and defend us. Beseech Almighty God to scatter like smoke the hosts of the wicked, who are seeking to destroy souls. Omnipotent God, take the matter into Thine own hands. Protect the souls which Thou hast created to Thine own image and likeness, for Thine enemies are bent on wresting them from Thee. Give us ever holy bishops, and priests, multiply the number of fervent religious, of apostolic men, of courageous and devoted Christians. Kindle in all hearts the sacred fire of zeal. O thrice holy God, let offences cease, convert sinners. Let all acknowledge Thee as the only true God, let all adore Thee and love Thee, in and with Jesus Christ, and grant, that there may be one fold and one Shepherd.

At the Agnus Dei.

Lamb of God, who takest away the sins of the world, have mercy upon us.

Lamb of God, who takest away the sins of the world, have mercy upon us.

Lamb of God, who takest away the sins of the world, grant us Thy peace.

At the Domine non sum dignus.

Jesus, my Saviour, can any love be compared to Thine? Thou didst consummate Thy sacrifice upon the Cross; Thou dost renew it in our hearts. O my Divine Redeemer, is it possible that Thou shouldst choose a miserable heart like mine as Thine Altar? O God of all holiness, Thou art coming to dwell in my heart. Truly I am not worthy, I am only a sinner. Nevertheless unworthy as I am, speak but a word, O God Almighty, and Thy servant's soul will be healed.

Before Communion.

Come O Lord, come my God who givest Thyself to us so freely. Give me Thy Sacred Flesh, and Thy Precious Blood. Give me Thy Heart, O Sweetest Jesus. Come into my soul to be its salvation, its strength, and its consolation in this valley of tears. Abide in me, and let me abide in Thee. Come, for my soul longs ardently for Thee. What can I desire in heaven or on earth, but to possess Thee, the God of my heart, and my portion for ever? (After your Communion, adore, love and contemplate your Blessed Lord Jesus, who is really present in your heart.

Pray to Him, and employ these precious moments in showing Him your love and gratitude, in asking abundant graces for yourself, for your relations, for the eighty thousand who are dying to-day, and whom I entreat you constantly to remember in your prayers, especially after Communion.)

Spiritual Communion.

(If you cannot have the happiness of receiving Holy Communion, made a Spiritual Communion, saying the following prayer, with humility and fervour.)

Jesus my Saviour, since I cannot to-day partake of the Bread of angels, give me at least the precious crumbs, which fall from Thy Table. I confess that I am not worthy of so great a favour, but I long for it, and I humbly beg it from Thee. Take away, I beseech Thee, every thing that makes me unworthy. Come, Lord Jesus, take possession of my heart and join it most closely to Thine. Come, my love, my life, my treasure, my joy; come, for I cannot live without Thee.

At the last Prayers.

O Jesus, guard the graces which Thou hast bestowed on me during this sublime sacrifice. Let me never be ungrateful for such love. Imprint upon my heart the remembrance of Thy benefits and the fear of Thy judgments; give me a sincere desire to please Thee, an unlimited confidence in Thy mercies, and a firm purpose to suffer death a thousand times rather than offend Thee once. Amen.

At the Benediction.

Bow down your head, and receive the Benediction of the priest, signing yourself with the sign of the Cross.

At the last Gospel.

Eternal Word, only Son of God, I thank Thee that Thou hast become man to make us the children of God. I also thank Thy Heavenly Father, and the Holy Spirit. What an honour and happiness it is for me to be called, and to be a child of God! O Jesus, give me grace to correspond to this glorious name by imitating the virtues of Thy Divine Heart, by conforming my dispositions to Thine, by treading in Thy steps along the path of humility, patience, mortification and charity. Take courage, my soul, I will be a faithful child of God while on earth, by-and-bye in heaven I shall be His heir, and a fellow-heir with Jesus Christ His Divine Son. Amen.

Before you leave the Church, return thanks to our Lord for the Holy Sacrifice at which you have assisted, pray Him to forgive your distractions, and make the following offering of your day to Him:

Sacred Heart of my Jesus, Victim of love sacrificed for me, I thank Thee for the mysteries which Thou hast now wrought for my salvation. I beg Thy forgiveness for any failings or negligences of which I have been guilty. I offer Thee an humble reparation for all those which have been committed this day during Holy Mass in any part of the world.

And now I go cheerfully to the employments to which Thou callest me. I offer them to Thee, O Sacred Heart, with every suffering Thou mayest please to send me. Let them all tend to Thy Glory, to my own growth in holiness, and to the salvation of my brethren, especially of those who are to die to-day. I unite my intentions and dispositions to Thine; direct me, and sanctify me. Give me an efficacious grace to preserve me henceforth from the sin into which I fall most constantly; deliver me from my imperfections; make me more patient, more humble, more gentle, more obedient, more charitable; take from me the love of worldly pleasures; strengthen me against all temptations; keep me from every sin; make me steadfast in faith and hope, and transform me into Thyself by love, so that my heart may be one with Thine, O my Jesus, to whom with the Father and Holy Spirit be all honour, love and glory, world without end. Amen.

CERTIFICATE OF ADMISSION.

Association of the Agonizing Heart of Jesus.

*On the ...... of the year of grace 18... M......
desiring to honour the Agonizing Heart of
Jesus with a special worship, and to do all in
her power for the salvation of those who die
each day, was received as a member of the
Association of the Agonizing Heart of Jesus,
established in the Church of N ...... at N......*
The Director.
The President.
The Secretary.

TICKET OF INTERCESSION.

*M...... is requested to make the half-hour's
Intercession for the dying, in the Church of
the confraternity of the Agonizing Heart of
Jesus, and to offer her communion for the same
intention, on the ...... 18...*

SIMULTANEOUS EXERCISE

*Of Perpetual Intercession to the Agonizing
Heart of Jesus, and Perpetual Supplication
to the Compassionate Heart of Mary.*

We beg those pious persons who are in the habit of making half-an-hour's intercession monthly for the dying, to add to their intercession the supplication of which we are about to speak. The closest affinity exists between the Agonizing Heart of Jesus and the Compassionate Heart of Mary, between the sorrows of the Son, and the sorrows of the Mother, therefore it is most fitting that these two devotions should never be separated, each will help the other, and their united fruits will be most abundant.

The object of *the Perpetual Intercession* to the Agonizing Heart of Jesus, is in the first place, to honour the Heart of Jesus in the sufferings which it endured for our salvation throughout His whole life, and especially in the Garden of Olives and on the Cross; and in the second place, by the merits of that long agony, to obtain the grace of a good death for the eighty thousand who die each day.

The object of the Perpetual Supplication to the Compassionate Heart of Mary, is in the first place, to honour the Heart of Mary in the sufferings which it endured for our salvation throughout her whole life, and especially while her Son was in agony in the Garden of Olives and on the Cross; and secondly, by those sufferings to obtain a great abundance of graces for the Church, for our country, for our neighbourhood, and for the hundred thousand children who are born each day.

The Simultaneous Exercise of Intercession and

THE AGONIZING HEART OF JESUS. 169

Supplication is made by at least two persons in the same Church. One kneels before the picture of the Agonizing Heart of Jesus, and makes intercession for the eighty thousand who are dying that day, while the other makes her supplication before the picture of the Compassionate Heart of Mary, for the need of the Church, for her country, for the town or neighbourhood in which she lives; and for the hundred thousand children who are born that day, that they may receive holy baptism and become good Christians.

This exercise lasts half-an-hour, and is generally performed from half-past-two to three o'clock in the afternoon. The day after that assigned for an Associate's *Intercession*, she should make the *Supplication*. A circle consists of thirty-one persons, and each circle should daily furnish two members, one to make intercession to the Agonizing Heart of Jesus, and the other to make supplication to the Compassionate Heart of Mary; one hour would thus be claimed from each associate every month. If, however, which God forbid, this be found too great a burden, the two devotions might be practised alternately; the same person making half-an-hour's intercession one month, and half-an-hour's supplication the next; the zelatrix should distribute the tickets accordingly, and arrange that the day after each associate's intercession, half-an-hour's supplication should be made by a member of the same circle: each associate should in this case extend her intention to all who are to be born or to die within the next forty-eight hours. But it would be far better if each associate could devote half-an-hour every month to the intercession, and half-an-hour to the supplication. Her intention would then only extend to the next twenty-four hours. We shall give the form of Tickets of Intercession and Supplication.

The prayers to be made during the time of Intercession have already been pointed out, others suitable for the time of Supplication will be found in a little book which we have published; "La Supplication perpétuelle au Cœur compatissant de Marie"...(Lécoffre, libraire, rue Bonaparte, Paris.)

We are indebted to the kindness of the late excellent Father Philip de Villefort, who died at Rome on the 26th of November, 1866, for two pictures of the Agonizing Heart of Jesus and the Compassionate Heart of Mary, they are the work of Chevalier Gagliardi, one of the ablest painters in the eternal city. Many copies have been made for other churches, and we shall be happy to give farther information to any one who may wish to apply to us.*

* Address, M. Gonnard; prêtre, au petit Seminaire, Sarlat Dordogne.

In many churches where it is impossible to have two separate chapels dedicated to the two Sacred Hearts, one might be dedicated to both together. In this case the two pictures should be placed in the most convenient manner for the simultaneous Intercession and Supplication. Prie-dieu chairs, and cards containing the necessary prayers, should also be provided.

The *Simultaneous Exercise* of which we have spoken may be begun by ten persons, the number should gradually and carefully be increased to thirty-one, which forms a complete circle. An intelligent and active zelatrix should be at the head of each circle, or one zelatrix may have several circles under her care. The co-operation of the parish priest, or, if the exercise is to be established in a religious house, of the superior or chaplain is necessary. The happiest results may be expected from this devotion.

We earnestly hope that where established, a solemn exercise of intercession may be made, by permission of the ordinary, on the Friday after Septuagesima,* and a solemn exercise of supplication on the following day.

All the faithful should be invited to assist; the devotions to be used on the day of intercession have been given in a previous chapter; others suited for the second day will be found in the

---

* On this day, in some countries, the Prayer of our Lord in the Garden is celebrated with a Mass and Office.

book we have referred to, "La Supplication perpetuelle."

Those persons who have the pious habit of frequently spending half-an-hour or an hour in adoration before the Blessed Sacrament, might with the greatest advantage devote a part of this time to alternate intercession and supplication. This will in no degree interfere with the homage they are paying to our Lord, and great blessings will be gained for the Church, for their country, for the parish or congregation to which they belong, for the dying, and the infants for whom they pray. We beg the clergy of churches where the Perpetual Adoration is established, and the Presidents of Confraternities which have that object in view, to take this matter into consideration, and to bring it before the members of these holy Associations. Tickets for intercession and supplication might be distributed along with those for the Perpetual Adoration, and copies of the Perpetual Intercession and the Perpetual Supplication might be left in the church for the use of those who practise these Devotions.

We have a firm conviction of the immense value of the *apostolic element* in all practices of piety; masters of the spiritual life well know its good results. The thought of our salvation, that is to say, the apostolic element, entered largely into all our Saviour's prayers. Its importance cannot be too strongly impressed upon the faithful, that they may learn to turn their accustomed prayers and works of piety to account in promoting the salvation of souls. The gain to their own souls will be great, for there is much merit in God's sight in caring for our neighbour's spiritual welfare as we do for our own. No virtue is more pleasing to God than charity; and is it not an eminent work of charity to make intercession to the Agonizing Heart of Jesus for the eighty thousand who die each day, to make supplication to the Compassionate Heart of Mary for the Church in her present distresses, for the Sovereign Pontiff, for England, etc., and for the hundred thousand children born each day, that they may receive holy baptism, and be preserved from the corruption of the world?

Alas! in these latter days, in the very heart of once Catholic Europe, wicked men have arisen and have assumed the infernal mission of making their fellow creatures die as reprobates, by keeping the priest away from the death-bed. And as if this impious cruelty were not enough, they deprive the children of baptism, so that they may grow up heathens. Christians, do not such dreadful things awaken your zeal? Surely you will not merely *intercede* for the dying, but will visit them, speak to them of God, and the salvation of their souls, induce them to admit the priest, and do all in your power to facilitate his entrance, and their reception of the Sacrament.

Surely you will not only make supplication for the Church, for the Sovereign Pontiff, for your country, and your neighbourhood, but you will endeavour to do good by every means in your power. You will not merely pray for the hundred thousand children who are born each day, but if you have the opportunity, you will use every effort to obtain baptism and a Christian education for those who are exposed to danger from the indifference or unbelief of their parents.

Daily Prayer to the Compassionate Heart of Mary for the 100,000 children who are born each day.

O clementissima Maria, Mater nostra, obsecro te per dolores Cordis tui Sanctissimi, per agoniam et per mortem dilectissimi Filii tui Jesu, lava in ejus Sanguine et serva semper in ejus corde dulcissimo et in tuo omnes infantes hodie nascituros. Amen.

O most merciful Mary, our mother, I entreat thee, by the sufferings of thy most holy Heart, by the agony and death of thy beloved Son Jesus, to cleanse in His Blood and to preserve for ever in His most loving Heart and in thine own, all the children who are to be born this day. Amen.

THE AGONIZING HEART OF JESUS. 175

Cor Mariæ, compassione plenum, ora pro infantibus hodie nascentibus.	Heart of Mary, full of compassion, pray for all the children to be born this day.

TICKET OF INTERCESSION AND OF SUPPLICATION.

M...... is requested to make in the chapel of the Association: 1st. Half-an-hour of Intercession to the Agonizing Heart of Jesus, the ... day of ......—2nd. Half-an-hour of Supplication to the Compassionate Heart of Mary, the ... day of......

ASSOCIATION OF VOLUNTARY VICTIMS.

Before concluding this book we will say a few words about the Association of Voluntary Victims for the needs of the church and the nations, especially the Catholic nations of Europe. This is not to be confounded with the preceding one; but as they owe their origin to the same feeling of compassion for the sorrows of our Holy Mother the Church, and of apprehension of the many dangers which beset souls in the present day, we bring its claims before those who have already undertaken the Intercession and Supplication. By joining the Association of Voluntary Victims they will carry out at once the apostolate of prayer, and the apostolate of suffering. Our Saviour's whole life on earth was the unbroken union of these two apostolates. He always prayed, therefore He always performed the office of an intercessor and suppliant; He always suffered, therefore He was always a victim, and in this manner He wrought the salvation of the world. Make intercession and supplication after His example, and you will be apostles of prayer. Offer yourselves as victims, patiently accept pains, sickness, tribulation, and death itself, for the good of the church and of souls, and you will become the apostles of suffering, and will co-operate with Jesus Christ in the salvation of souls.

A touching example of this double Apostolate was recently given by Father Philip de Villefort, a holy religious of the Society of Jesus, whose charity is well known to French Catholics, especially to priests who have been in Rome; he died at Rome on the 26th November, 1866, after having made a voluntary offering of his life to God for the Church. Would that our words might stir up some ardent souls to follow in his steps! It is written of our Divine Saviour, He was offered because it was His own will. *Oblatus est quia ipse voluit.* If He shall lay down His life for sin, He shall see a long-lived seed. *Si posuerit pro peccato animam suam, videbit semen longævum.* Because His Soul hath laboured, He shall see and be filled. *Pro eo quod laboravit anima ejus, videbit et saturabuntur.* He shall divide the spoils of the strong, because He hath delivered His Soul unto death, and was reputed with the wicked. *Fortium dividet spolia pro eo quod tradidit in mortem animam suam et cum sceleratis reputatus est.* (Is. liii.) Imitate our Divine Master's self-devotion. Offer yourselves with Him and like Him as victims for souls, and at length you will have part in His glory and His eternal triumph. You will gain souls, and throughout all eternity you will be rewarded for the prayers you have made and the suffering you have borne on their behalf.

We do not doubt that many who have undertaken the work of Perpetual Intercession and Supplication will be led by their great love of God, and their desire for His glory and the salvation of souls also to enrol themselves in the Association of Voluntary Victims.

We therefore give the series of Tickets used by this Association, taken from our book, "The Apostolate of Suffering," which may be found useful to members.

ASSOCIATION TICKETS

Of the Voluntary Victims for the needs of the Church and the Nations, especially the Catholic Nations of Europe, in honour of the Agonizing Heart of Jesus, and of the Compassionate Heart of Mary.

This Association consists of pious persons, devoted to the glory of God and the salvation of souls, who offer in common, all their works, their pains, their sufferings, and the sacrifice of their life itself, to obtain for the Church and the nations, especially the Catholic nations of Europe, a great abundance of spiritual help in these evil days. They propose to pay special honour to the agony and death of Jesus Christ, and to the sufferings of His Blessed Mother, and to offer themselves daily as *victims* for the Church and nations, especially their own, and that named on the ticket assigned to them. They become as *victims* by offering to God their afflictions, their pains, and *above all their life;* by accepting with patience the sufferings which come upon them, by asking God to let them suffer more for the Church and the Nations, if such be His good pleasure. Consequently none but devoted Christians, who are ready to *suffer*, and if need be, to *die* for the interests of Jesus Christ, of His Church, of the Sovereign Pontiff, and of souls, should enter this Association. As to its organization, it simply consists in bringing together ten persons who are prepared to carry out this practice. Every second month, one of them distributes to the others the following tickets. When a member dies, the survivors pray for the departed soul, and fill up the vacant place.

FIRST TICKET.

The Church and France.

Honour the Agony and Death of Jesus Christ, and the interior and exterior sufferings which He endured from the moment of His incarnation until the age of five years, more especially at the thought of all the children who should be born of infidels, heretics, or bad Catholics.

In union with these sufferings, offer your works, your sufferings, and the sacrifice of your life for the triumph of the Catholic Religion in France, for fathers and mothers of families, and for children, that they may receive baptism and preserve their baptismal innocence. Ask God, if such be His good pleasure, that you may suffer for these intentions.

Agonizing Heart of Jesus, have mercy on us.
Compassionate Heart of Mary, pray for us.
Saint Michael, archangel, pray for us.
Holy Guardian angels of France, pray for us.

St. Joseph, pray for us.
Holy Apostles and Martyrs, pray for us.
Saints who have sanctified yourselves in France, pray for us.

SECOND TICKET.

The Church and Italy.

Honour the Agony and Death of Jesus Christ, and the interior and exterior sufferings which He endured from the age of five to ten years, especially at the thought of all the children brought up in forgetfulness of God and in contempt for our Holy Religion.

In union with these sufferings, offer your works, your pains, your sufferings, and the sacrifice of your life for the triumph of religion in Italy, and especially for all children, that they may receive a Catholic education. Ask God, that if such be His good pleasure, you may suffer for these intentions.

Agonizing Heart of Jesus, have mercy on us.
Compassionate Heart of Mary, pray for us.
Saint Michael, Archangel, pray for us.
Holy Guardian Angels of Italy, pray for us.
St. Joseph, pray for us.
Holy Apostles and Martyrs, pray for us.
Saints who have sanctified yourselves in Italy, pray for us.

THIRD TICKET.

The Church and Spain.

Honour the Agony and Death of Jesus Christ, and the interior and exterior sufferings He endured from the age of ten to fifteen years, especially at the thought of the many young Christians who go astray at that age.

In union with these sufferings, offer your works, your pains, your sufferings, and the sacrifice of your life for the triumph of the Catholic religion in Spain and Portugal, especially for the complete extirpation of the causes of scandal which pervert youth, such as bad books, bad newspapers, and bad plays. Ask God, if such be His good pleasure, that you may suffer for these intentions.

Agonizing Heart of Jesus, have mercy on us.
Compassionate Heart of Mary, pray for us.
Saint Michael, Archangel, pray for us.
Holy Guardian Angels of Spain and of Portugal, pray for us.
Saint Joseph, pray for us.
Holy Apostles and Martyrs, pray for us.
Saints who have sanctified yourselves in Spain and Portugal, pray for us,

FOURTH TICKET.

The Church and Austria.

Honour the Agony and Death of Jesus Christ, and the interior and exterior sufferings He endured from the age of fifteen to twenty years, especially at the thought of the many young Christians of both sexes, who do not follow their vocation, and who from their unfaithfulness are in danger of being lost.

In union with these sufferings, offer your works, your pains, your sufferings, and the sacrifice of you life for the triumph of the Catholic religion in Austria and Hungary, for all religious, for Christian youth, particularly for students. Ask of God, if such be His good pleasure, that you may suffer for these intentions.

Agonizing Heart of Jesus, have mercy on us.
Compassionate Heart of Mary, pray for us.
Saint Michael, Archangel, pray for us.
Holy Guardian Angels of Austria and Hungary, pray for us.
St. Joseph, pray for us.
Holy Apostles and Martyrs, pray for us.
Saints who sanctified yourselves in Austria and in Hungary, pray for us.

FIFTH TICKET.

The Church and Germany.

Honour the Agony and Death of Jesus Christ, and the interior and exterior sufferings which He endured from the age of twenty to twenty-five years, especially at the thought of the frightful evil which secret societies and bad company do to the youths and men of the present day.

In union with these sufferings, offer your works, your pains, your sufferings, and the sacrifice of your life for the triumph of the Catholic religion in Germany and Russia, and especially for workmen, for youths, and other persons, that they may not enter secret societies, and that these bad associations may be extirpated. Ask of God, if such be His good pleasure, that you may suffer for these intentions.

Agonizing Heart of Jesus, have mercy on us.
Compassionate Heart of Mary, pray for us.
Saint Michael, Archangel, pray for us.
Holy Guardian Angels of Germany and Russia, pray for us.
St. Joseph, pray for us.
Holy Apostles and Martyrs, pray for us.
Saints who sanctified yourselves in Germany and in Russia, pray for us.

SIXTH TICKET.

The Church and England.

Honour the Agony and Death of Jesus Christ, and the interior and exterior sufferings which He endured from the age of twenty-five to thirty years, especially at the thought of the persons of that age, who abandon themselves without restraint to their disordered passions.

In union with these sufferings, offer your works, your pains, your sufferings, and the sacrifice of your life for the triumph of the Catholic religion in England, Ireland, and Scotland, particularly for those who govern in these countries and elsewhere. Ask of God, if such be His good pleasure, that you may suffer for these intentions.

Agonizing Heart of Jesus, have mercy on us.
Compassionate Heart of Mary, pray for us.
Saint Michael, Archangel, pray for us.
Saint Joseph, pray for us.
Holy Apostles and Martyrs, pray for us.
Holy Guardian Angels of England, Ireland, and Scotland, pray for us.
Saints who sanctified yourselves in these three kingdoms, pray for us.

SEVENTH TICKET.

The Church and Poland.

Honour the Agony and Death of Jesus Christ, and the interior and exterior sufferings which He endured from the age of thirty to thirty-three years, especially at the thought of the many persecutions His Church should undergo till the end of time.

In union with these sufferings, offer your works, your pains, your sufferings, and the sacrifice of your life that the Catholic religion may triumph in Poland, and in all the countries in the world in which it is persecuted, and that the confusion of Babel may fall upon all the enemies of the Church, so that they may become unable to hurt her. Ask of God, if such be His good pleasure, that you may suffer for these intentions.

Agonizing Heart of Jesus, have mercy on us.
Compassionate Heart of Mary, pray for us.
Saint Michael, Archangel, pray for us.
St. Joseph, pray for us.
Holy Apostles and Martyrs, pray for us.
Holy Guardian Angels of Poland, and of other nations where the Catholic Church is persecuted, pray for us.
Saints who sanctified yourselves in Poland and

in those countries where the Church is persecuted, pray for us.

EIGHTH TICKET.

The Church and Belgium.

Honour the Passion and Death of Jesus Christ, and the interior and exterior sufferings which He endured in the Garden of Olives during the three hours of His Agony, especially at the thought of the great number who die daily under God's anger.

In union with these sufferings and this dolorous Agony, offer your works, your pains, your sufferings, and the sacrifice of your life for the triumph of the Catholic religion in Belgium, Holland, Sweden, Norway, and Denmark, and especially for the 80,000 who die each day, and for the complete extirpation of the abominable sect of solidaires,* whose infernal object is to keep the dying from dying as Christians. Ask of God, if such be His good pleasure, that you may suffer for these intentions.

    Agonizing Heart of Jesus, have mercy on us.
    Compassionate Heart of Mary, pray for us.
    Saint Michael, Archangel, pray for us.
    Saint Joseph, pray for us.
    Holy Apostles and Martyrs, pray for us.

    * This wicked sect has lately arisen in Belgium.

Holy Guardian Angels of Belgium and the other nations of the North of Europe, pray for us.

Saints who sanctified yourselves in Belgium and the other Northern countries, pray for us.

NINTH TICKET.

The Church and America.

Honour the Agony and Death of Jesus Christ, and the interior and exterior sufferings which He endured during His Scourging and Crowning with Thorns, especially at the thought of the spiritual independence of so many men, who refuse to submit themselves to His Divine Authority, and that of His Holy Spouse, the Church.

In union with these sufferings, offer your works, your pains, your sufferings, and the sacrifice of your life for the triumph of the Catholic religion in America and Oceanica, and especially for all missionaries. Ask of God, if it be His good pleasure, that you may suffer for these intentions.

Agonizing Heart of Jesus, have mercy on us.
Compassionate Heart of Mary, pray for us.
Saint Michael, Archangel, pray for us.
Holy Guardian Angels of America and Oceanica, pray for us.

Saint Joseph, pray for us.

Holy Apostles and Martyrs, pray for us.

Saints who sanctified yourselves in America and Oceanica, pray for us.

TENTH TICKET.

The Church. Asia, and Africa.

Honour the Agony and Death of Jesus Christ, and the interior and exterior sufferings which He endured in bearing His Cross, in being crucified on it, in hanging on it for three hours, and in giving up the ghost, though He foresaw the ingratitude of so many men who would not benefit by the merits of His Blood there shed for them.

In union with these sufferings, offer your works, your pains, your sufferings, and the sacrifice of your life for the triumph of the Catholic religion in Asia, Africa, and all heathen countries, and particularly for the Sovereign Pontiff, for bishops, priests, and all children of the Holy Catholic Apostolic Roman Church, especially for the members of this Association, for their families and your own. Ask of God, if such be His good pleasure, that you may suffer for these intentions.

Agonizing Heart of Jesus, have mercy on us.

Compassionate Heart of Mary, pray for us.
Saint Michael, Archangel, pray for us.
Holy Guardian Angels of Asia, Africa, and all the countries in the world, pray for us.
St. Joseph, pray for us.
Holy Apostles, pray for us.
Holy Martyrs and Virgins, pray for us.
Saints who sanctified yourselves in Asia, Africa, and all the countries in the world, pray for us.

Note.—Letters asking information regarding the Confraternity and Association of the Agonizing Heart of Jesus, etc., can be addressed to P. Lyonnard, at the Petit Séminaire de Sarlat (Dordogne), or to Madame La Supérieure des Réligieuses du Cœur Agonizant de Jesus, à Lyon, quartier de Monplaisir, aux Quatre Maisons, No. 11. A Confraternity and Association of the Agonizing Heart of Jesus have been established in the Church of this Community, and those who wish can join it. (Prepay all applications.)

Praised be the Agonizing Heart of Jesus.
Praised be the Compassionate Heart of Mary.

THE END.